THE ESSENTIAL
MIDDLE EASTERN
COOKBOOK

THE ESSENTIAL
MIDDLE
EASTERN
COOKBOOK

Classic
Recipes
Made
Easy

MICHELLE ANDERSON

Photography by
Helene Dujardin

**ROCKRIDGE
PRESS**

For general information on our other products and services or to obtain technical support, please contact our Customer Care Department within the United States at (866) 744-2665, or outside the United States at (510) 253-0500.

Rockridge Press publishes its books in a variety of electronic and print formats. Some content that appears in print may not be available in electronic books, and vice versa.

TRADEMARKS: Rockridge Press and the Rockridge Press logo are trademarks or registered trademarks of Callisto Media Inc. and/or its affiliates, in the United States and other countries, and may not be used without written permission. All other trademarks are the property of their respective owners. Rockridge Press is not associated with any product or vendor mentioned in this book.

Interior and Cover Designer: Amanda Kirk
Art Producer: Michael Hardgrove
Editor: Mo Mozuch
Production Editor: Jenna Dutton

Photography © 2020 Helene Dujardin. Food styling by Anna Hampton.
Pages 13, 18: art used under license from © Shutterstock.com.
On the cover: Persian Stew with Walnuts and Pomegranate (Fesenjan)

ISBN: Print 978-1-64611-638-6 | eBook 978-1-64611-639-3

R1

**TO MY BOYS,
MAC AND COOPER.**

• • •

*Your willingness to try
every food once,
even octopus tentacles
when 10 and 7 years old,
is inspiring and fuels
my creativity.*

CONTENTS

•••

INTRODUCTION

Welcome to the deeply traditional, incredibly flavorful world of Middle Eastern cooking! I was introduced to the region because my father worked extensively throughout the Middle East for several decades. As a teenager, I joined him and my mother for extended visits. After becoming a chef, I worked throughout North Africa, learning about the cuisine as a professional, rather than hailing from it as a local.

I received lessons about how to cook flavorful stews, dips, and mouthwatering desserts from tiny giggling women who did not speak a word of English, and I stocked my kitchens with the most abundant, fresh ingredients I have ever had the pleasure of using as a chef. When I returned to my home in Canada to continue my career, I became part of a flourishing fusion movement that added Middle Eastern elements to many restaurant dishes. The flavors, recipes, and techniques from the region were hot and trendy, and patrons could not get enough.

The recipes in this book reflect decades of learning and cooking the food that inspires me the most. I endeavored to respect the ingredients and preparations, while creating dishes that do not take days to produce or use foods that are not available in North America. As a result, you should have no problem creating incredible cuisine that will inspire you, as well.

You will first learn a little about the Middle East, including the different regions that make up this part of the world and the rich culinary history of each. We will then explore the various spices and pantry items that you will need to create the recipes within this cookbook. Soon, you will be preparing Middle Eastern cuisine with confidence!

Sabich,
page 93

Chapter One

THE MIDDLE OF EVERYWHERE

The descriptor "Middle East" was introduced at the end of the 19th century. From a European perspective, it described the area that was east of Europe, but was not the Far East. Regions are defined by many factors, such as physical and geological boundaries—including seas and mountains—and more nebulous influences such as shared languages, religions, and history. In the case of the Middle East, all of these factors come into play to specify the regional area.

Within the Middle East, there are sub-regions, including the Levant, Persia, the Fertile Crescent, the Arabian Peninsula, and North Africa. The Middle East is incredibly diverse—in language, religion, culture, and history—so the food of this region is vibrant and often overlaps in techniques, ingredients, and actual recipes. Maps sometimes differ in how they outline countries considered to be in the Middle East, but generally (and for the purpose of this book) they include the following:

Bahrain	Jordan	Palestine	Turkey
Cyprus	Kuwait	Qatar	United Arab
Iran	Lebanon	Saudi Arabia	Emirates
Iraq	Oman	Syria	Yemen
Israel			

North Africa also has a strong culinary influence on the Middle East, specifically as it pertains to the following countries:

Egypt	Libya	Morocco	Tunisia

The Culinary Regions of the Middle East

The Middle East is a complex and vibrant area with a very pronounced culinary personality. There are, of course, differences in ingredients and techniques within the different countries and regions, but you will also find an abundant overlap of recipes. Sometimes a recipe is essentially identical, but with a different spelling of the name, and other times there is a twist on the ingredients that reflects the region. While many are regionally unique, some dishes and spice blends that overlap across the Middle East include the following:

- **Baba Ghanouj** (page 27)
- **Bahārāt** (page 147)
- **Baklava** (page 126)
- **Couscous** (pages 42 and 55)
- **Falafel** (page 28)
- **Fattoush** (page 47)
- **Harissa** (page 148)
- **Hummus** (page 26)
- **Kanafeh** (page 135)
- **Kebab** (page 105)
- **Labneh** (page 25)
- **Lentil Soup** (page 66)
- **Maqluba** (page 111)
- **Muhammara** (page 31)
- **Mujadarra** (page 44)
- **Pita** (page 22)
- **Ras El Hanout** (page 151)
- **Shakshuka** (page 81)
- **Shawarma** (page 119)
- **Tabbouleh** (page 45)
- **Tahini** (page 142)
- **Tagine** (pages 110 and 116)
- **Torshi** (page 29)
- **Za'atar** (page 146)

THE LEVANT—CYPRUS, ISRAEL, JORDAN, LEBANON, PALESTINE, SYRIA, AND TURKEY

The Levant is home to many cultures, religions, and climates. It is also home to some of the most delicious food in the world. Agriculture has thrived in this area for almost 10,000 years, so the variety of ingredients is impressive. Conquests, changes in rulers, and immigration have also created many culinary influences.

Dietary laws can also dictate or influence food choices and combinations. An example of this would be kashruth (keeping kosher) in Israel, which means milk and meat cannot be included in the same meal, meat must come from animals with cleft hooves, and pork is not eaten. Animals must be slaughtered a certain way, and there are also rules surrounding shellfish and flesh-eating birds.

Levantine cuisine has something for everyone, whether one consumes meat or is pescatarian, vegetarian, or vegan. Meals are created with fresh ingredients and are often served as a mezze, which is a variety of small dishes, both hot and cold, sometimes served as the actual meal or as an appetizer.

Typical regional ingredients and culinary offerings include the following:

- **Proteins** such as lamb, beef, chicken, and turkey that are roasted, marinated, skewered, and stewed, stuffed into vegetables and grape leaves, and then served with lemons and herbs, or tahini-based sauces. Fish and poultry are also popular choices. Other protein sources include dairy products such as yogurt, feta, halloumi, goat cheese, eggs, and cream.

- **Fresh produce** such as eggplant, zucchini, garlic, olives, pomegranates, citrus fruit, dates, figs, grape leaves, tomatoes, green beans, artichokes, cabbage, onions, tomatoes, and peppers, as well as fresh herbs such as mint, parsley, cilantro, oregano, and dill.

- **Legumes and grains** such as chickpeas, lentils, fava beans, wheat, rice, and bulgur. Fresh bread and flatbread are also common with most meals.

- **Nuts and seeds** such as almonds, pine nuts, pistachios, sesame seeds, and walnuts.

- **Spices** such as allspice, nutmeg, cinnamon, cumin, coriander, sumac, turmeric, caraway, cardamom, and a spice blend called Bahārāt.

PERSIA AND THE FERTILE CRESCENT—IRAN, IRAQ

The Fertile Crescent is named for the shape this area makes on the map: a crescent of farmland marked by the Tigris and Euphrates rivers. As with other regions in the Middle East, many influences converge to create a vibrant, diverse cuisine. Due to its position on the Silk Road trade route, you will see the imprint of the Levant, Greece, Russia, Asia, Europe, Turkey, and India on the recipes of Persia and the Fertile Crescent. Ingredients valued by other countries are indigenous to Iran, where the four-season climate is favorable to grapes, oranges, nuts, pomegranates, and coveted saffron.

Some typical ingredients of the region's cuisine include the following:

- **Proteins** such as lamb, goat, beef, chicken, turkey, eggs, and fish.

- **Fresh produce** such as pumpkins, onions, garlic, carrots, tomatoes, cucumbers, scallions, eggplant, grapes, melons, pomegranates, turnips, beans, shallots, okra, citrus fruit, cherries, dates, olives, dark leafy greens, potatoes, cabbage, zucchini, apples, lettuces, leeks, figs, artichokes, peppers, and chiles.

- **Legumes and grains** such as chickpeas, lentils, rice, bulgur, wheat, and barley.

- **Dairy,** including yogurt, cream, milk, feta, and halloumi.

- **Nuts and seeds,** including pistachios, walnuts, sesame seeds, almonds, hazelnuts, and pine nuts.

- **Spices and fresh herbs** such as sumac, parsley, cinnamon, cardamom, oregano, coriander, mint, fenugreek, cumin, thyme, saffron, dill, and turmeric, and blends such as Bahārāt and za'atar.

THE ARABIAN PENINSULA—BAHRAIN, KUWAIT, OMAN, QATAR, SAUDI ARABIA, UAE, YEMEN

There is a distinct international food influence running through the cuisine in this region due to the flourishing expatriate communities and tourism in the larger urban centers. You can find almost any type of food, from traditional to Western franchise restaurants, including plenty of Indian dishes such as dal and curries created with imported ingredients such as coconut milk.

In Arabian Peninsula recipes, you will find the following:

- **Proteins** such as lamb, chicken, beef, goat, and fish. Pork is an uncommon ingredient because it is prohibited (*haram*) under Islam, which is the predominant religion of the region.

- **Fresh produce** such as zucchini, onions, garlic, potatoes, artichokes, dark leafy greens, carrots, okra, dates, pomegranates, citrus fruit, melons, grapes, stone fruit, and olives.

- **Legumes and grains** such as chickpeas, lentils, bulgur, semolina, rice, wheat, peas, fava beans, lupini beans, and runner beans are prevalent. Bread is part of almost every meal, whether pita or wheat loaves.

- **Dairy products and eggs** are used generously, especially yogurt, butter, cheese, and cream.

- **Nuts and seeds** such as almonds, pistachios, sesame seeds, pine nuts, walnuts, and peanuts.

- **Popular herb and spice** choices include parsley, cilantro, saffron, sumac, black pepper, turmeric, cardamom, cinnamon, nutmeg, chili, paprika, cumin, coriander, cloves, and ginger, as well as blends such as Bahārāt, za'atar, and Ras El Hanout.

North Africa is not geographically part of the Middle East, but from a culinary perspective, these countries have had a strong impact. The food from this region is popular in other parts of the world because it features what can be considered clean or whole-food eating, with fresh fruits and vegetables, legumes, grains, lean fish and meats, nuts, and seeds. Recipes are shaped by ingredients, geography (coastal, plains, or desert), way of life (city, rural, or nomadic), and outside influences such as trade, immigration, and proximity to other countries.

Libyan and Moroccan cuisines have strong European themes. For example, Libya has many pasta dishes. However, unlike Italian pasta, Libyan cooks throw dry pasta right into sauces to cook, rather than boiling it in water. Moroccan cuisine is very eclectic and has complex flavors due to its long interaction with other countries. Egypt has spicy dishes but not necessarily hot food; its cuisine is a lovely blend of many Middle Eastern regions because of the spice trade routes. Tunisia has the fieriest cuisine, with many different influences combining to create multi-faceted food with French, Jewish, Arab, and Italian themes.

Ingredients in North African food are quite similar across the various countries, with a few variations:

- **Proteins** include lamb, goat, chicken, duck, goose, eggs, camel, and pigeon in various forms such as ground, stuffed, grilled, stewed, and served raw in some recipes. Pork is considered *haram* (forbidden) and is not readily available in most regions.

- **Legumes, grains, vegetables, and fruits** are staple ingredients in many recipes. North African cuisine uses chickpeas, red kidney beans, fava beans, lentils, bulgur, wheat, millet, semolina, rice, corn, barley, onions, garlic, eggplant, tomatoes, green beans, zucchini, carrots, okra, dark leafy greens, chiles, cauliflower, potatoes, dates, figs, apples, mangos, oranges, limes, lemons, peaches, apricots, cherries, melons, grapes, and olives.

- **You will also see** almonds, pistachios, hazelnuts, sesame seeds, chestnuts, peanuts, pine nuts, pecans, yogurt, cheeses, olive oil, bread, couscous, honey, fresh herbs, fresh ginger, and a vast range of spices in North African recipes.

- **Floral waters and fruit essences** are also common in desserts.

The Other Mediterranean Diet

The Mediterranean diet is popular these days as one of the healthiest choices for anyone looking to make a lifestyle change. The food is packed with familiar ingredients and evokes images of Greece or Italy, or other areas along the Mediterranean Sea. In fact, the Mediterranean diet is influenced by 21 countries, several of which actually *are* on the Mediterranean Sea, such as Libya, Tunisia, Egypt, Morocco, Lebanon, Turkey, Israel, and Syria. The earliest crops and produce were cultivated in these lands, and they were also integral to the earliest culinary trade.

Pita bread dates back thousands of years and has its origins in Mesopotamia, an ancient area that roughly covers modern-day Iraq, with parts of Turkey, Iran, and Syria. Pita bread remains a Middle Eastern staple today. It is thought that Bedouins traveling the deserts spread this flatbread through the Middle East to North Africa and then to the Mediterranean countries beyond. Falafel, hummus, kefir, tahini, harissa, and many spices are now staple items in grocery stores all over the world and are often considered to be "Mediterranean diet" ingredients when, in fact, they are Middle Eastern in origin. These gateway foods are introducing people to the rich culture and delightful flavors of the Middle East and awakening an appreciation for the traditional cuisine that is part of this area of the world.

Street Eats

Street food in the Middle East has gained such international fame that it is a tourist attraction and can be found in food trucks and carts in New York, London, and Toronto. Walk by a row of them, and the scent of the piquant spices and roasting meat will surely draw you in closer. Now, imagine the intertwined aroma of several dozen different stalls, including that of bread baking in clay ovens hundreds of years old, which is eaten within two hours of baking. That is what it is like to experience true street eats.

Some of the most famous street food in the Middle East includes the following:

- **Falafel (page 28):** Falafel is stuffed into a warm pita with fresh chopped tomatoes, tangy pickles, and a scoop of cool yogurt. There are countless delicious variations of this recipe served all over the Middle East.

- **Koshari (page 95):** This Egyptian national dish is a hearty mixture of macaroni, rice, lentils, crispy fried onions, and a spicy sauce. It is typically assembled in bowls and served with flatbread to scoop up every wonderful bite.

- **Sabich (page 93):** This sandwich is served on countless street corners of major cities all over the world. It consists of a soft pita stuffed with crispy fried eggplant, chopped vegetables, hummus, hardboiled eggs, and tahini sauce.

- **Turkish Baked Potato (Kumpir) (page 46):** Foil-wrapped, piping hot potatoes are slit, and the tender steaming flesh is mixed in the potato skin with cheese until very soft and melty. Then you can choose toppings that include legumes, pickles, sauces, vegetables, meats, shredded poultry, cheeses, and olives. It tastes best eaten while standing up, trying hard not to burn your mouth.

- **Manakeesh (page 37):** This is the Middle Eastern version of pizza: crisp flatbread topped with vegetables, meats, cheeses, and a drizzle of hot sauce or tahini. It is healthier than North American pizza but equally addictive and delicious.

- **Kanafeh (page 135):** Found in the Levant region, this delicious selection consists of buttery, crisp pastry filled with gooey melted cheese and soaked in honey or syrup. If you are fortunate, the sweet treat will be topped with a scoop of cream and a scattering of chopped nuts.

- **Shawarma (page 119):** This delicacy consists of spiced, slowly grilled meats shaved off the spit and tucked into a pita, then topped with chopped cucumber, tomatoes, hummus, or tahini sauce.

The Spice of Life

Some of the most interesting and exhilarating aspects of Middle Eastern food are the spices. I remember visiting the spice market in Tripoli and catching the scent of the spices blocks away, the fragrance drifting on the warm air of the coastal city. As I turned the corner, the alley opened up into a large square, holding hundreds of spices along with the vendors entreating the teeming crowds to buy their wares. I spent several delightful hours selecting at least a dozen spices and waiting for them to be weighed on beautiful copper scales and poured into little cloth bags. I then hustled home with this treasure trove of new flavors, eager to try them in the kitchen.

Middle Eastern food is all about spices, combinations of textures, and a pleasing complexity of flavor that is often created through centuries of making a particular recipe or spice blend. This cuisine has roots and traditions. The following lists will give you an excellent start on the pantry items and spices you will need to create delicious food. Every spice in the following list can be found in your local grocery store, except for possibly sumac, which you might have to source online (see the resource section on page 153). You can also look for it in an international or Middle Eastern market, if you have one in your community. Spices lose their pungency, so either buy them whole and grind them yourself or check the dates on the jars and make sure the products are not past the "best before" date. You can also purchase spices in bulk. Store the spices in glass jars in a cool, dark, dry place. You might already have many of the items. If not, you do not have to go out and get everything in this section right away. Purchase what you need for a recipe and slowly build up to a fully stocked Middle Eastern pantry.

SPICE LIST

- **Allspice:** This spice is warm, slightly peppery, and similar to a blend of cinnamon, black pepper, cloves, and nutmeg. It can be used effectively in both sweet and savory recipes and is quite strong, so a little goes a long way. In Middle Eastern food, allspice is used in many traditional dishes, such as Fasulia (page 64), Bazella Riz Lahme (page 60), and Kibbeh (page 107).

- **Anise (Aniseed):** The anise plant is believed to originate from Egypt and is one of the oldest spices in the world. Its strong licorice flavor is distinctive and similar to fennel seeds, star anise, and caraway seeds. It is used in desserts, stews, broths, and meat recipes.

- **Bay leaves:** This herb originates from the laurel tree. The leaves don't have much flavor or scent until they are steeped in a soup, stew, or other liquid. When they are, they display flavors that are woodsy and slightly mentholated, and they will help bring out the flavors of other herbs and spices. The leaves are usually removed before the dish is eaten.

- **Caraway seeds:** This member of the carrot family has a licorice taste similar to cumin, aniseed, fennel seeds, and nigella seeds. This spice was common in ancient Egypt and often prized for its medicinal uses, such as relieving digestive complaints. Caraway is popular in North African dishes, vegetable recipes, and bread making and is found in some cheeses.

- **Cardamom:** This spice is herbal, almost flowery, with hints of citrus, pepper, and eucalyptus. Complex and potent, cardamom does not have a comparable substitute, but in a pinch, you can use a combination of cinnamon and cloves or nutmeg to create a similar flavor profile. Cardamom is used in Middle Eastern dishes and spice blends such as Shawarma Spice (page 149) and Bahārāt (page 147).

- **Cayenne pepper:** This hot spice is usually used in powder form and comes from a dried chile pepper often found in South America. You can substitute red pepper flakes, hot Spanish paprika, or a dash of Tabasco, but these ingredients will add different flavor components to the dish.

- **Cinnamon:** Made from the inner bark of trees, cinnamon is one of the most commonly used spices. It is prized for its warm, aromatic, and almost sweet flavor. This spice is used in powdered form as well as in whole sticks. If you do not have cinnamon on hand, try substituting a smaller quantity of allspice in the recipe.

- **Cloves:** Originating from the flower buds of an Indonesian evergreen tree, this spice is used in both powdered and whole forms. Cloves have an intense flavor, almost hot, with warm, sweet undertones. Nutmeg and allspice are good substitutes for cloves.

Cloves are used in spice mixes, desserts, and in many meat recipes.

- **Coriander:** Coriander is the dried seeds of the fresh herb plant cilantro. This aromatic spice has a warm, sweet flavor with a bit of citrus accent. If you do not have coriander, try caraway seeds or cumin in the same amount. Coriander is a primary spice in many Middle Eastern and North African blends such as Ras El Hanout (page 151) and Bahārāt (page 147).

- **Cumin:** This pungent, warm, citrusy spice comes from a Middle Eastern plant belonging to the parsley family. In a pinch, you can substitute coriander or caraway seeds, but it is best to keep this spice handy. Cumin is used in Falafel (page 28), Shawarma (page 119), and many soups, stews, and dips.

- **Fennel seeds:** This spice displays flavors that are warm and sweet, with a licorice undertone that is not as pungent as aniseed, which can be a good substitute. The seeds are often found in savory and sweet dishes and are common in sausage recipes such as Spiced Beef Sausage (Merguez) (page 113).

- **Ginger:** This spice is warm, hot, and sweetish in flavor, which makes it a lovely addition to savory and sweet dishes. Dried ginger is a versatile spice because it retains its flavor even when cooked at high temperatures, so it is wonderful for marinades, grilled meats, or tagines. Allspice and mace make good choices as alternatives to ginger.

- **Mint:** Mint (most commonly spearmint) has a cool, sweet menthol flavor commonly paired with meats such as lamb, in dips, and famously in Tabbouleh (page 45). If you don't have mint in your kitchen, try basil instead. It is not the exact same flavor but is complementary.

- **Paprika:** These dried, smoked ground peppers, originating from Central America, can be mild and sweet, or fiery hot. Paprika imparts strong flavor and color to food, including Bahārāt (page 147), Çiğ Köfte (page 92), and Shakshuka (page 81). A good alternative to hot paprika is cayenne pepper.

- **Peppercorns:** Peppercorns are the dried fruit of a flowering vine, commonly found as black, white, and green, depending on when they are picked and processed after harvesting. North African cuisine also uses long peppercorns and grains of paradise.

- **Red chili flakes:** The heat in many Middle Eastern dishes is complex rather than just mouth scorching. Some of the commonly found Middle Eeastern red chili flakes are maras pepper flakes, rich and mild-tasting; or Aleppo pepper, moderately hot. Chili flakes are used as a garnish in soups, stews, marinades, and spice blends.

- **Saffron:** One of the most expensive spices in the world, saffron is nearly exclusively produced in Iran. Saffron threads should have a light-colored tip, so if the thread is one color, then it is a dyed stigma from a different flower. Saffron has a lovely sweet floral flavor and imparts a deep yellow color to your recipes. Common dishes for its use include Luqaimat (page 34), Kachi (page 86), and Tachin (page 97).

- **Sesame seeds:** While not actually a spice, they are included here because they are a very common flavor element in Middle Eastern cuisine. Sesame seeds are mild and nutty, but get richer in taste when toasted. Sesame seeds are used in tahini, as a garnish, and in desserts.

- **Sumac:** This spice will probably be the most difficult one to find outside of the Middle Eastern region. The berries and sometimes the leaves of the sumac bush are dried and ground to create a lemony, fruity-tasting spice. Suitable alternatives to sumac are lemon pepper seasoning, store-bought za'atar seasoning (it contains sumac), and plain lemon zest or juice. Sumac is found in Muhammara (page 31), Fattoush (page 47), and, of course, homemade Za'atar (page 146).

- **Turmeric:** This spice comes from the root of a plant related to ginger. It is slightly bitter and pungent, with a hint of ginger. The value of this spice is often the color it imparts to food such as rice, rather than its flavor profile. In the event that you require an alternative, ginger and cumin will probably come the closest.

Smoke 'Em If You Got 'Em

If you do a lot of cooking, it might be wise to consider purchasing whole spices for convenience and to save money. You can grind them straight from the jar, or else elect to toast the spices, which draws out and deepens the flavor. Toasting spices releases the oils: volatile (which provide the flavor), and non-volatile (which provide the aroma).

There are several methods for toasting spices, but the method I prefer is as follows:

1. Preheat a small, heavy-bottomed skillet over medium-low heat and add the whole spices. Swirl the spices around the skillet until they become fragrant, about 2 minutes. Some spices will jump or pop as they heat up.
2. Slide the toasted spices onto a plate or into a bowl and let them cool completely.
3. Grind the spices using a spice or coffee grinder, or with a mortar and pestle. You can store toasted spices in a sealed jar in a cool, dark place for up to 2 weeks, but they are best used the same day you toast them. If you are going to store them, leave the spices whole until you use them in a recipe.

Best spices for toasting include the following:

Cardamom

Cinnamon

Coriander seed

Cumin seed

Fennel seed

Mustard seed

Star anise

On Your Grind

Spices are a crucial addition to most Middle Eastern recipes. Grinding your own means purchasing whole spices rather than ground versions of the same ingredient. You can buy a good spice grinder either at a kitchen store or online for about $25.00, and if you clean and maintain it well, it should last years. Grinding your spices will cause an accumulation of oils in the blades and bowl over time. This can ruin the taste of freshly ground spices, especially when stronger spices overpower the more delicate ingredients. Grinders usually cannot be immersed in water, so the best cleaning method is a dry one. Put either uncooked rice or pieces of stale bread in the grinder and pulse until the ingredients are pulverized. Then, discard the rice or crumbs and wipe out the grinder with a damp towel. To remove any lingering scent, pour two tablespoons of baking soda in the grinder and grind for about one minute. Dump out the baking soda and wipe again with a damp cloth.

Pantry Staples

- **Basmati or other long-grain rice:** Rice is an essential ingredient in Middle Eastern cuisine. Basmati rice has a wonderful nutty, almost floral fragrance and extra-long grains that cook to a fluffy texture that does not clump together. Basmati comes in both white and brown varieties and does not have to be soaked. You can use other long-grain rice in place of basmati, but that marvelous unique taste will not be present.

- **Bulgur:** Consisting of whole wheat berries that are parboiled, dried, and cracked (which means it cooks quickly), this ingredient is chewy and has a lovely nutty flavor that combines well with other ingredients. It is the base ingredient in Tabbouleh (page 45), Kisir (page 48), and Kibbeh (page 107). Quinoa and freekeh can be used as a substitute for bulgur.

- **Chickpeas:** This legume has many names, such as Egyptian pea, garbanzo bean, or Bengal gram, and is the main ingredient in many Middle Eastern recipes such as Hummus (page 26). It is firm and buttery tasting, and when it's pureed, it is velvety and luxurious. Chickpeas can be found in Falafel (page 28), Vegetable Harira Soup (page 69), and Ash-e Bademjan (page 75).

- **Couscous:** Couscous is often thought to be a grain, but it is actually a pasta made from coarse semolina. It can be combined with stews, sauces, and dressings and will soak up the taste of all the accompanying ingredients.

- **Dried fruits (raisins, dates, apricots, cherries):** Dried fruit is a popular ingredient in Middle Eastern cuisine. Drying or dehydrating fresh produce such as dates, grapes, and figs ensures the preservation of quality and concentration of natural sugars. Some traditional recipes that use dried fruit are Maamoul (page 128), Tbit (page 122), and Masoub (page 79).

- **Filo dough:** Filo or phyllo dough, from the Greek *phyllon,* meaning "leaf," is a paper-thin unleavened flour dough that is used in many traditional recipes, such as Baklava (page 126) and Börek (page 84).

- **Ghee:** Ghee is butter that is cooked over very low heat to lightly caramelize the milk solids, and then strained to remove all water. This creates a shelf-stable oil with a high smoke point and a rich, nutty flavor. This process also removes the elements in butter that affect those who are sensitive to dairy: the lactose and casein.

- **Honey:** Honey is an ancient essential ingredient in cooking that takes on the flavor of the flowers frequented by the bees. Honey is a key component in many Middle Eastern dishes such as Luqaimat (page 34), Masoub (page 79), and Baklava (page 126).

- **Lemon juice:** Lemons are a staple of Middle Eastern cuisine in the form of juice, zest, and often as a preserved whole fruit. Adding lemon to a dish will sharpen the flavors, including spices and herbs.

- **Lentils:** These legumes have been cultivated for centuries and are the base of many traditional Middle Eastern recipes such as Koshari (page 95), Mujadarra (page 44), and Salata Adas (page 50). Lentils come in different colors, such as yellow, red, and green, with red lentils being the sweetest and most likely to lose their texture when cooked.

- **Limes, dried:** Dried limes are used in stews, soups, broths, and tagines, and are placed in the cavity of chickens and whole fish before roasting.

- **Nuts (pistachios, almonds, walnuts, and pine nuts):** Nuts are an essential ingredient in the Middle East. Crunchy, green-hued, slightly sweet nuts are used in desserts, in pilafs, and as a topping or stuffing in savory and sweet dishes. Walnuts are another popular nut and may be found in Muhammara (page 31), Kashke Bademjan (page 32), and Fesenjan (page 59).

- **Olive oil:** The oil of choice in Middle Eastern cooking, it is even drizzled over finished dishes to add flavor and texture, such as with Hummus (page 26) or Harissa-Roasted Cauliflower (page 57). Olive oil comes in different grades that vary in flavor, odor, and acidity. Avoid exposing olive oil to air, heat, and light to ensure your oil stays fresh and flavorful.

- **Orzo:** *Orzo* is Italian for "barley." This small pasta is made with semolina flour and is traditionally used in soups, salads, and pilafs.

You can try orzo in Tabbouleh (page 45) or Kisir (page 48) instead of bulgur.

- **Pine nuts:** Pine nuts (pignoli) are the small, pale seeds of pine trees. They have a light buttery taste and are soft when raw, so they are often toasted to provide a little crunch. Pine nuts are used as a tasty topping, in desserts, and often in Hummus. You can find them in Lebanese Hashweh (page 114), Maqlooba (page 111), and Tachin (page 97).

- **Plain Greek yogurt:** Yogurt is a popular food in the Middle East by itself, as a topping, as a dip, stirred into soups and stews, and even as the base for a strained cheese called Labneh (page 25).

- **Pomegranate syrup/molasses:** A reduction of pure pomegranate juice that can be purchased or self-prepared (see page 74), this ingredient is a gorgeous red color, is intensely flavored but not sweet, and has been used for thousands of years in Middle Eastern recipes. You can use it in Fesenjan (page 59), Muhammara (page 31), or marinades, dressings, and glazes for meats and poultry.

• **Tahini:** This thick paste is made from ground, hulled sesame seeds, either toasted or plain. You can either buy this nutty, rich ingredient or make it yourself with sesame seeds and oil in a food processor. Tahini is typically used in sauces (page 142), Baba Ghanouj (page 27), and Hummus (page 26).

• **Semolina flour:** Semolina is flour made from durum wheat, also called macaroni wheat and pasta wheat. This type of wheat is mostly cultivated in the Middle East. Semolina is coarser and darker (almost golden) in color, and has a slightly stronger scent than regular wheat flour. Semolina is used in couscous, puddings such as Mamounieh (page 132), and Baghrir (page 87).

• **Sugar:** Desserts are very popular in the Middle East. They are a traditional part of the meal, and many desserts have attar or sweet sugar syrup as a component. This syrup consists of sugar dissolved in water and simmered until it thickens slightly. Sometimes this syrup is flavored with rose water or lemon juice. Sugar syrup is used in Kachi (page 86), Baklava (page 126), and Mamounieh (page 132).

• **Vegetable oil:** Olive oil is often the preferred oil choice, but other vegetable oils are used. Sesame oil, almond oil, sunflower oil, and walnut oil are all good options for dressings and for frying, depending on the recipe. You can also use coconut oil if you have it in your pantry, but it is not a traditional choice.

Chickpea Check-Up

Canned legumes can be very high in sodium and other additives, even if you drain and rinse them. To get the healthiest, high-quality ingredient, try cooking your own chickpeas. To do so, I suggest the following steps to cook 2 cups of dried chickpeas:

- Carefully sift through the dried beans and remove any rocks, inedible bits, and damaged beans.
- Pre-soak the chickpeas. This will ensure the beans cook quicker and are easier to digest. Put the chickpeas in a medium bowl with ¼ teaspoon baking soda and cover with about 2 inches of water. Soak overnight. The baking soda will help the chickpeas soften when cooked.
- Drain the chickpeas, rinse in cold water, transfer to a medium saucepan, and then cover the beans again in about 3 inches of water and place on medium-high heat.
- Bring the water to a boil, reduce heat to low, partially cover the pan, and simmer until the beans are tender but still retain their shape, about 1½ to 2 hours. Check for foam while the chickpeas are simmering and skim it off when it collects on the top.
- Drain the water and set the chickpeas aside to cool for 30 minutes. Transfer the chickpeas to a plastic bag (do not seal) or a container and set in the refrigerator until completely cool. Then seal the bag, after pressing out all the air, or cover the container.
- Store the cooled chickpeas in the refrigerator in a sealed plastic bag or container for up to 4 days or spread the cooled beans on a baking sheet in a single layer and freeze. Then transfer the frozen chickpeas to a plastic bag, press out the air, seal, and store in the freezer for up to 3 months.

About the Recipes

The recipes included in this book are meant to introduce you to the incredible ingredients and dishes of the Middle East and to allow you to make the favorites you have enjoyed in restaurants or from street vendors. Care was taken to include many dishes from each region and to respect the traditions that surround each meal. Some of the ingredients have been altered to reflect availability, and some techniques have been simplified so that the recipes are accessible to a home cook who is interested in, but not may not be familiar with, Middle Eastern cuisine.

Most of the recipes in this book are clearly labeled to help you choose dishes that suit individual and family needs, diet, or tastes, as well as available time and energy. The following labels are included to help you navigate the recipes quickly and easily:

- **Quick and Easy:** These are recipes you can throw together in about 30 minutes. The techniques and ingredients are uncomplicated. They are perfect when you are in a time crunch and still want a delicious meal or snack.

- **Vegetarian:** There are many types of vegetarian diets, depending on what you want to restrict and the reason you follow the diet. The recipes in this book assume a lacto-ovo approach to the diet, so they include dairy products, eggs, and honey, but do not include meat or seafood.

- **One-Pot:** These are the recipes in this book that are constructed in a single skillet, saucepan, bowl, baking dish, or stockpot.

Pita Bread, page 22
Hummus, page 26

Chapter Two

SPREADS AND SNACKS

I f you are a Middle Eastern food enthusiast, this chapter will probably contain the most familiar dishes in the book. You will find pita bread, garlicky hummus, baba ghanouj, and golden falafel in this section. Until fairly recently, these foods were not easily obtainable products and had to be prepared from scratch in one's own kitchen, or else enjoyed in a local restaurant. Now, most grocery stores sell prepared hummus and packaged pita bread. Making your own is still best because you can adjust the ingredients to suit your own palate and control what goes into the finished product.

Pita Bread

MAKES 8 ♦ **PREP TIME:** 40 minutes, plus rising time ♦ **COOK TIME:** 24 minutes

I remember the first time I successfully made pita bread; several attempts created delicious but very flat bread. Watching the bread puff up in the oven was a personal triumph. This recipe might look complicated, but once you get the hang of the steps and what to look for concerning rise, you will be turning out perfect pitas all the time.

1 cup warm water (105°F to 110°F)

1 tablespoon olive oil, plus extra for greasing the bowl

1 package (2¼ teaspoons) instant yeast

2 teaspoons sugar

1 teaspoon sea salt

3 cups all-purpose flour, divided, plus extra

1. In a medium bowl, stir together the water, oil, yeast, sugar, salt, and ½ cup flour with a wooden spoon until smooth.

2. Stir in the remaining 2½ cups flour until the dough comes together into a rough ball.

3. Knead the dough in the bowl until it is smooth and elastic, adding pinches of flour if needed to stop the dough from sticking, 8 to 10 minutes. Form the dough into a smooth ball.

4. Grease a large bowl with olive oil and set the ball of dough in the bowl, turning it to coat the dough in oil. Cover the bowl with a clean, damp kitchen cloth and set aside in a warm place to rise for 1 hour.

5. Punch the dough down and place it on a lightly floured surface, kneading a few times. Cut the dough into 8 equal pieces, forming each piece into a ball.

6. Cover the pieces with the damp cloth and let them sit for 15 minutes.

7. Roll each ball into a 6-inch circle about ¼ inch thick, cover with damp cloths, and let rise for 30 minutes.

8. Preheat the oven to 500°F and put a baking sheet in the oven to heat up.

9. Place two pitas at a time on the baking sheet, close the oven door, and bake until the pitas are puffed and lightly golden, 2 to 3 minutes.

10. Remove the cooked pitas to a towel-lined plate, wrapping them completely.

11. Repeat with the remaining pitas, working quickly so that the heat is not lost from the oven.

12. Serve immediately.

13. Store any leftover pitas in a sealed plastic bag in the refrigerator for up to three days.

COOKING TIP: Consider investing in a baking or pizza stone rather than using a baking sheet. This cooking tool holds and transfers heat well, so the steam release that creates the signature dough pocket is more effective.

Serbian Roasted Eggplant Pepper Spread (Ajvar)

SERVES 4 ♦ **PREP TIME:** 15 minutes ♦ **COOK TIME:** 40 minutes

When roasted red bell peppers are combined with eggplant, garlic, and herbs, you get a multi-hued, versatile spread that is easy to prepare and undeniably appetizing. You can substitute yellow and orange bell peppers in a pinch, but the color will be less vibrant.

1 large eggplant

3 red bell peppers

2 tablespoons olive oil

1 tablespoon white vinegar or freshly squeezed lemon juice

1 teaspoon minced garlic

1 teaspoon chopped fresh parsley

Sea salt

Freshly ground black pepper

1. Preheat the oven to 450°F.

2. Place the eggplant and red peppers on a baking sheet and roast until the vegetables are lightly charred, turning several times, about 20 to 25 minutes.

3. Transfer the vegetables to a large bowl and cover it tightly with plastic wrap. Let the vegetables sit for 15 minutes to allow the steam to loosen the skins.

4. Take the vegetables out, peel off the skins, and remove the seeds and stems from the peppers.

5. Put the vegetables in a food processor along with the olive oil, vinegar, garlic, and parsley and pulse until chopped but not pureed.

6. Transfer the mixture to a medium saucepan and bring to a boil over medium-high heat.

7. Reduce the heat to low and simmer to thicken and combine the flavors, about 15 minutes.

8. Remove from the heat and season with salt and pepper.

9. Let cool to room temperature and serve.

10. Store in a container in the refrigerator for up to 1 week.

COOKING TIP: To save time, you can use store-bought roasted red peppers instead of making your own. Most large jars contain at least three full peppers.

Lebanese Cream Cheese (Labneh)

SERVES 4 ♦ **PREP TIME:** 10 minutes, plus draining time

As an 18-year-old, I watched with what can only be described as disdain as my mother set up bowls of straining yogurt in her kitchen in Zanzur, Libya. What on earth was she doing when you could buy cheese at the market? As with most things, she was right. The finished cheese was tart and velvety, with just the right amount of salt to perk up the taste buds.

| 8 cups plain yogurt | ¼ to ½ teaspoon sea salt | 2 to 3 tablespoons olive oil |

1. Line a large colander with cheesecloth and set it over a large bowl.
2. In a medium bowl, stir together the yogurt and salt and transfer to the colander.
3. Put the bowl and colander in the refrigerator and let the yogurt drain off its liquid for 12 to 24 hours. The mixture will be quite firm, similar to goat cheese.
4. Squeeze the cheese to remove any remaining liquid, transfer it to a medium bowl, and stir in the olive oil.
5. Store covered in the refrigerator for up to 1 week.
6. Save the liquid yogurt whey (kashk) in another container

VARIATION TIP: You can strain this recipe for longer and roll the drier cheese-like product in herbs or spices.

Hummus

SERVES 4 ♦ **PREP TIME:** 10 minutes

Hummus is a dish that used to be obscure and relegated to ethnic menus, but during the last 20 years, this humble dip has become mainstream and can now be found in most grocery stores. However, making your own is simple, and you can adjust the flavor and ingredients to suit your palate. Try using different legumes, a handful of greens, and herbs and spices to create delicious variations on this basic recipe.

1 (15-ounce) can
  sodium-free chickpeas,
  drained and rinsed
¼ cup freshly squeezed
  lemon juice

2 tablespoons tahini
2 teaspoons minced garlic
Sea salt
2 tablespoons olive oil

1 teaspoon chopped
  fresh parsley, for
  garnish (optional)

1. Put the chickpeas, lemon juice, tahini, and garlic in a blender or food processor.
2. Blend until smooth, occasionally scraping down the sides of the appliance, 2 to 3 minutes.
3. Season with salt.
4. Transfer to a small bowl and drizzle with olive oil.
5. Top with parsley (if using) and serve with pita bread or vegetables.
6. Store in a container in the refrigerator for up to 1 week.

FUN FACT: There are records of hummus recipes that date back more than 7,000 years, making this dish one of the oldest in the world!

Eggplant Dip (Baba Ghanouj)

SERVES 4 ♦ **PREP TIME:** 15 minutes ♦ **COOK TIME:** 25 minutes

As a child, I was never an eggplant fan. Little did I know it was the recipe or skill of the cook that determined the palatability of this delightful vegetable. Roasted eggplant has a gloriously creamy texture and a rich taste that combine beautifully with smoky tahini and the sharpness of lemon. You can use this as a dip or spread, or eat it by the tablespoon right out of the container.

1 large eggplant

Juice of 1 lemon

2 tablespoons tahini

1 tablespoon olive oil

2 teaspoons minced garlic

Sea salt

Freshly ground
   black pepper

1 tablespoon chopped
fresh parsley

1. Preheat the oven to 450°F.

2. Place the eggplant on a baking sheet and roast until it is lightly charred, turning several times, 20 to 25 minutes.

3. Transfer the eggplant to a large bowl and cover it tightly with plastic wrap. Let the eggplant sit for 15 minutes to allow the steam to loosen the skin.

4. Peel off the skin and put the eggplant in a food processor, along with the lemon juice, tahini, olive oil, and garlic.

5. Pulse until slightly chunky and well combined and season the dip with salt and pepper.

6. Top with chopped parsley and store in a container in the refrigerator for up to 5 days.

VARIATION TIP: If you crave a Persian creation, add a teaspoon each of ground coriander and cumin to the recipe in step 4.

Falafel

SERVES 4 ♦ **PREP TIME:** 25 minutes, plus overnight soaking time ♦ **COOK TIME:** 5 minutes

Falafel is one of those never-fail creations. It coaxes complex flavors from simple ingredients. Serve your falafel tucked into pitas with shredded lettuce, chopped tomato, and a spoonful of tangy yogurt sauce. You can also top these delicious patties with Tahini Sauce (page 142) or Hummus (page 26).

1 cup dried chickpeas, rinsed and picked through

½ small sweet onion, finely chopped

2 tablespoons all-purpose flour

2 tablespoons finely chopped fresh parsley

2 teaspoons minced garlic

1½ teaspoons ground cumin

1 teaspoon ground coriander

½ teaspoon sea salt

¼ teaspoon freshly ground black pepper

Pinch allspice

Olive oil, for frying

1. Put the chickpeas in a medium bowl and cover with about 3 inches of water. Soak overnight.

2. Drain the chickpeas, then transfer them to a food processor and pulse a few times.

3. Add the onion, flour, parsley, garlic, cumin, coriander, salt, pepper, and all-spice and pulse to form a thick paste. Chill the mixture in the refrigerator for 15 minutes.

4. Roll the mixture into 1½-inch balls and flatten them slightly.

5. Heat 1 inch of oil in a large skillet over medium-high heat until about 350°F.

6. Fry the patties until golden brown, turning once, about 3 minutes in total.

7. Transfer the patties to a paper-towel-lined plate and serve.

8. Store any leftover patties in a container in the refrigerator for up to 3 days.

SUBSTITUTION TIP: You can also use canned chickpeas for this recipe. Use a 15-ounce can instead of dry chickpeas, and skip step 1.

Pickled Vegetables (Torshi)

SERVES 4 ♦ **PREP TIME:** 25 minutes, plus standing time ♦ **COOK TIME:** 5 minutes

Pickles are a worldwide culinary creation. There are very few countries that do not have their own variation on this dish. This recipe is not as sour as some popular pickles due to the added sugar, so if you prefer a more vinegary taste, reduce the sugar to 2 tablespoons.

½ head cauliflower, cut into small florets

2 large carrots, peeled and cut into ½-inch rounds

1 cup green beans, cut into 3-inch pieces

1 fresh chile pepper, seeded and cut into small slices

3 garlic cloves, crushed

3 sprigs parsley

½ cup white vinegar

¼ cup granulated sugar

2 bay leaves

¼ teaspoon caraway seeds or coriander seeds

Pinch sea salt

1. Bring a medium pot of water to a boil over high heat. Blanch the cauliflower for 2 minutes, then drain and rinse with cold water.

2. Put the florets in a large bowl and add the carrots, green beans, chile pepper, garlic, and parsley. Stir to combine and set aside.

3. In a small saucepan, stir together the vinegar, sugar, bay leaves, caraway seeds, and salt and set over medium heat.

4. Bring the marinade to a simmer, stirring frequently. Then, reduce the heat to low and simmer for 5 minutes to dissolve the sugar and infuse the vinegar with the herbs and spices.

5. Remove the bay leaves and pour the marinade over the vegetables, tossing to combine.

6. Cover the bowl and let it stand for 6 to 8 hours.

7. Store leftovers in a container in the refrigerator for up to 1 week.

VARIATION TIP: Experiment with different vegetables and different amounts of brine ingredients, such as more vinegar for a Persian-style pickle and more salt for a Turkish version.

Pita with Za'atar

SERVES 4 ♦ **PREP TIME:** 10 minutes ♦ **COOK TIME:** 6 minutes

Sometimes the most straightforward combination of ingredients, such as flatbread and seasoning, creates a satisfying meal. This dish is more a snack than a full-course offering, but it is filling. Try cutting the finished pita into strips and serving it with a yogurt garlic dip, Hummus (page 26), or Baba Ghanouj (page 27).

4 pita breads	2 tablespoons za'atar
3 tablespoons olive oil	Pinch sea salt

1. Preheat the oven to 350°F.

2. Line a baking sheet with parchment paper.

3. Carefully cut the pita breads open, creating two rounds from each bread. Place the pita bread smooth side down on the baking sheet.

4. In a small bowl, stir together the oil, za'atar, and salt.

5. Brush the cut sides of the pitas with the oil mixture.

6. Bake the pitas until lightly golden, about 6 minutes.

COOKING TIP: Try creating this dish on a grill on medium heat for a lovely charred flavor. Brush the pita with the oil and spice mixture and grill, turning once, for about 3 minutes in total.

Roasted Red Pepper Dip (Muhammara)

SERVES 4 ♦ **PREP TIME:** 10 minutes

My mother was born in Indonesia, so we often had meals that consisted of many small dishes, called Rijsttafel. This dip would have felt at home on our "rice table," as it does on a Middle Eastern mezze platter. Muhammara is a gorgeous color and is quite thick as a result of the bread crumbs and walnuts.

1 (6-ounce) jar roasted red peppers, drained

½ cup bread crumbs

½ cup chopped walnuts

2 tablespoons olive oil

1 tablespoon freshly squeezed lemon juice

1 teaspoon minced garlic

1 teaspoon ground cumin

½ teaspoon sumac (optional)

⅛ teaspoon sea salt

Pinch red pepper flakes

1. Put red peppers, bread crumbs, walnuts, olive oil, lemon juice, garlic, cumin, sumac (if using), salt, and red pepper flakes in a food processor and pulse until smooth and well combined.

2. Store in a sealed container in the refrigerator for up to 5 days.

COOKING TIP: If you cannot find sumac in your grocery store or specialty market, ½ teaspoon lemon zest can stand in for 1 teaspoon sumac.

Persian Eggplant Dip

SERVES 4 ♦ **PREP TIME:** 20 minutes ♦ **COOK TIME:** 36 minutes

The taste of kashke bademjan is quite different from the more well-known Baba Ghanouj (page 27) because of the walnuts, mint, and kashk. If you are not a fan of other eggplant dips, try this one.

3 tablespoons olive oil, divided

3 eggplants, peeled and halved lengthwise

½ sweet onion, thinly sliced

2 teaspoons minced garlic

½ teaspoon turmeric

¼ teaspoon sea salt

¼ cup water

½ cup chopped walnuts, divided

1 tablespoon chopped fresh mint

½ cup kashk (see last step in Lebanese Cream Cheese [Labneh]) (page 25)

½ cup Crispy Fried Onions (page 145)

1. Heat 2 tablespoons of olive oil in a large skillet over medium-high heat. Add the eggplants to the skillet, cut-side down, and sear until softened and golden brown on all sides, turning several times, about 12 minutes.

2. Transfer the eggplants to a plate and set aside. Add the remaining 1 tablespoon of oil to the skillet and sauté the onion and garlic, stirring frequently, until lightly caramelized, about 8 minutes.

3. Stir in the turmeric and salt, and sauté 1 minute more.

4. Stir in the water and add the eggplants back to the skillet. Bring to a boil and reduce the heat to low, partially cover the skillet, and simmer until the eggplant is very tender, about 15 minutes.

5. Remove from heat and pulse till smooth in a food processor with ¼ cup walnuts.

6. Transfer the dip to a serving bowl and top with the mint, kashk, remaining ¼ cup of walnuts, and crispy fried onions.

7. Serve or store in a sealed container in the refrigerator for up to 4 days

---

COOKING TIP: Kashk can be purchased online in liquid or dry form.

Yogurt and Cucumber Dip (Mast-o Khiar)

SERVES 4 ♦ **PREP TIME:** 15 minutes

Cucumber, yogurt, and mint are a classic combination of flavors, fresh and tangy all at once. The raisins add a wonderful burst of sweetness, both unexpected and pleasing.

½ cup golden raisins

1 cup plain yogurt

1 cucumber, shredded with the liquid squeezed out

2 teaspoons minced fresh mint

1 teaspoon minced garlic

Sea salt

Dried rose petals, for garnish (optional)

1. Put the raisins in a small bowl and cover with warm water until very tender, about 10 minutes. Drain and transfer half the raisins to a medium bowl and stir in the yogurt, cucumber, mint, and garlic.

2. Season the dip with salt.

3. Garnish with the remaining raisins and rose petals (if using).

4. Serve or store in a container in the refrigerator for up to 3 days.

MENU TIP: This refreshing tart dip can be served with warm flatbreads or spooned over meats, poultry, and fish. Try it with Iraqi Yellow Spice-Rubbed Chicken (page 118), Lamb Köfte (page 92), or Masgouf (page 99).

Arabic Sweet Dumplings (Luqaimat)

SERVES 4 ♦ **PREP TIME:** 30 minutes, plus rising time ♦ **COOK TIME:** 24 minutes

Luqaimat means "bite-size" in Arabic, a good description for these crunchy, golden-fried, and honey-drizzled dumplings. Just make sure you serve the dumplings the same day you make them because they lose their delightful crunch overnight.

¾ cup warm water, divided

½ teaspoon cardamom powder

Pinch saffron threads

¼ cup sugar

½ package instant yeast (about 1 teaspoon)

2 cups all-purpose flour

¾ cup instant milk powder

Sunflower or vegetable oil, for frying

½ cup honey or date syrup

1. In a small bowl, stir together ¼ cup water, the cardamom powder, and the saffron and set aside for 10 minutes.

2. In another small bowl, stir together the remaining ½ cup water, sugar, and yeast and set aside for 10 minutes.

3. In a large bowl, stir together the flour and milk powder.

4. Add the cardamom mixture to the yeast mixture and stir to combine.

5. Stir the yeast mixture into flour until batter is smooth.

6. Cover the bowl with a clean cloth and let the dough rise until doubled and bubbly, 40 to 45 minutes.

7. In a large saucepan, heat about 4 inches of oil until it is about 350°F.

8. Drop the batter by tablespoons into the oil, frying for about 1 minute until the dumpling floats up and is light golden brown. Then turn it over to evenly fry the other side, about 1 minute more.

9. Remove the dumplings using a slotted spoon and place on a paper-towel-lined plate. Repeat with the remaining batter.

10. Arrange the dumplings in a bowl and drizzle with honey or syrup. Serve.

FUN FACT: Saffron is the most expensive spice in the world for good reason. It comes from the stigma of crocus flowers, and each flower has only three stigmas. It takes almost 5,000 flowers to produce one ounce of saffron threads!

Arabic Mutton Samosa (Sambousak)

SERVES 4 ♦ **PREP TIME:** 45 minutes ♦ **COOK TIME:** 35 minutes

Samosas are not just an Indian creation; they can be found in many countries. You can make these golden spicy packets with store-bought phyllo if you want to skip the dough steps in this recipe. This version uses ground lamb as the stuffing, but cheese, spinach, legumes, beef, and chicken all work.

For the dough

¼ teaspoon dry yeast

3 tablespoons warm water

1½ cups all-purpose flour

¼ teaspoon ground
   cardamom

¼ teaspoon sea salt

⅓ cup whole milk,
   at room temperature

2 tablespoons canola
   or sunflower oil

For the filling

2 tablespoons olive oil

½ pound extra-lean
   ground lamb

1 sweet onion, chopped

¼ teaspoon red chili flakes

¼ teaspoon ground
   cinnamon

2 tablespoons chopped
   fresh parsley

Vegetable oil, for frying

To make the dough

1. In a small bowl, stir together the yeast and water and set aside for 10 minutes.

2. In a medium bowl, mix together the flour, cardamom, and salt until well combined. Add the milk and oil and mix until combined.

3. Stir the yeast mixture into the flour-milk mixture until the dough is smooth and firm. Cover with a clean cloth and set aside while you make the filling.

To make the filling

1. Heat the oil in a large skillet over medium-high heat and sauté the lamb until cooked through, about 10 minutes.

2. Stir in the onion and sauté until lightly caramelized, about 5 minutes.

3. Stir in the chili flakes, cinnamon, and parsley and cook until all liquid is evaporated and the mixture is lightly browned and dry.

CONTINUED ▶

4. Remove from the heat and blot any grease from the mixture. Set aside to cool.

5. Lightly flour a work surface and roll the dough out to about ¼-inch thickness. Use a 4-inch pastry cutter or drinking glass to cut rounds out of the dough.

6. Top each dough round with about 2 teaspoons or 1 tablespoon of cooled filling and fold it over to form a half-moon. Crimp the edges closed with a fork or your fingertips. Repeat with all the dough.

7. Heat about 4 inches of oil in a large saucepan to 350°F and fry the sambousak in batches until golden, turning once, for 4 to 6 minutes in total. Transfer the cooked sambousak to a paper-towel-lined plate and repeat until all are cooked.

8. Serve.

VARIATION TIP: Israeli sambusaq (regional spelling) is filled with chickpeas, onions, and spices. Instead of frying, try brushing these pastries with an egg wash and baking them in a 350°F oven for about 40 minutes.

Lebanese Flatbread (Manakeesh)

SERVES 4 ♦ **PREP TIME:** 45 minutes, plus rising time ♦ **COOK TIME:** 7 minutes

In the late 1980s, I ordered what was described to me as "pizza" in a restaurant in Tripoli and got a flatbread topped with spices, cheese, and a sliced hardboiled egg. This was a version of manakeesh, and since then, I have enjoyed this dish much more than as a teenager.

1 cup warm water	3½ cups all-purpose flour,	¼ cup olive oil, plus extra
1 package (2¼ teaspoons)	plus extra for dusting	for greasing
dry active yeast	1 teaspoon sea salt	¼ cup grated mozzarella
		or akawi cheese

1. In a small bowl, stir together the water and yeast. Set aside for 10 minutes.

2. In a large bowl, stir together the flour and salt, then blend in the yeast mixture and oil and combine to form a soft dough.

3. Turn the dough out on a lightly flour-dusted surface and knead until it is elastic and smooth. If it is too sticky, add a little more flour.

4. Transfer the dough to a lightly oiled medium bowl and turn to coat in oil. Cover the bowl with a clean, damp cloth and let rise in a warm place for about 1½ hours.

5. Preheat the oven to 400°F.

6. Lightly oil a baking sheet and place it in the oven while the oven is heating. Carefully remove the baking sheet from the oven when the oven is hot.

7. Punch the dough down and roll it into a disc ¼ to ½ inch thick. Transfer to the hot baking sheet and sprinkle with the cheese.

8. Bake until lightly golden brown, 6 to 7 minutes.

9. Serve with Pickled Vegetables (page 29) or sliced tomato.

VARIATION TIP: Try this tasty bread with za'atar (page 146) topping for breakfast or minced meats, tomatoes, and spices for a more filling lunch or dinner.

Shanklish

SERVES 4 ♦ **PREP TIME:** 20 minutes, plus draining time ♦ **COOK TIME:** 15 minutes

When visiting one of my father's colleagues in Libya, I was ushered into the women's side of the house and sat with several ladies in the kitchen enjoying tea so thick and sugary you could stand a spoon up in it. On the shelves of the refrigerator were glass jars of what turned out to be flavorful shanklish. Don't let the straining time of this recipe intimidate you. It is very simple, and the resulting feta-like cheese is wonderful.

4 cups plain yogurt

¼ cup water

½ teaspoon red
 pepper flakes

¼ teaspoon smoked paprika

¼ teaspoon sea salt

¼ cup to ½ cup Za'atar
 (page 146), for rolling

Olive oil

1. In a large saucepan, stir together the yogurt, water, red pepper flakes, paprika, and salt and bring to a boil over medium-high heat.

2. Reduce the heat to low and simmer until the mixture resembles cottage cheese, about 15 minutes.

3. Line a large colander with fine-mesh cheesecloth and set it over a bowl.

4. Pour the curds and whey mixture into the colander and let it strain for about 2 hours at room temperature. Discard the liquid.

5. Pour the za'atar on a plate and set near the firm yogurt mixture.

6. Scoop out the yogurt mixture by tablespoons and roll into firm balls. Then roll the balls in the seasoning and set aside.

7. Repeat with the remaining mixture, and transfer the finished balls to a container.

8. Cover the balls with olive oil and store covered in the refrigerator for up to 2 months.

MENU TIP: This cheese can be eaten by itself as a tempting appetizer but is also wonderful crumbled and added as a topping to soups and salads, or mashed with hardboiled eggs and stuffed into a pita with fresh tomatoes and cucumber.

Israeli Couscous,
page 55

Chapter Three

SIDES AND SALADS

I first visited the Middle East when I was a teenager, and I was delighted to discover the best produce I have ever experienced. The vegetables and fruit were not sprayed with pesticides or fungicides to accelerate or delay ripening. They were juicy, unbelievably flavorful, and bursting with color and scent. The salads and sides in this section embrace the perfection of these ingredients and are prepared to highlight the various tastes and textures.

Moroccan Couscous with Roasted Vegetables

SERVES 4 ♦ **PREP TIME:** 25 minutes ♦ **COOK TIME:** 20 minutes

While this is not a traditional recipe, it was inspired by my time spent in Morocco. A citrus dressing and fresh mint topping boost the lovely flavor of the roasted vegetables and couscous. The addition of almonds and raisins adds crunch and an extra burst of sweetness to the finished dish. You can add any ingredient that you enjoy, such as halved cherry tomatoes, eggplant, pistachios, cucumber, and chopped herbs.

For the dressing

3 tablespoons olive oil

Juice of ½ lemon

1 teaspoon ground coriander

½ teaspoon ground cumin

¼ teaspoon ground cinnamon

Dash ground allspice

Sea salt

For the couscous

2 zucchini, cut into ¼-inch rounds

2 garlic cloves, lightly crushed

1 carrot, sliced

1 red bell pepper, diced

1 sweet onion, cut into 1-inch chunks

1 tablespoon olive oil

2 cups low-sodium chicken or vegetable broth

1 cup dry couscous

½ cup golden raisins

½ cup toasted sliced almonds

2 tablespoons chopped fresh mint

To make the dressing

1. In a small bowl, whisk together the olive oil, lemon juice, coriander, cumin, cinnamon, and allspice until well blended.

2. Season with salt and set aside.

To make the couscous

1. Preheat the oven to 400°F.

2. Line a baking sheet with parchment paper and set aside.

3. Arrange the zucchini, garlic, carrot, bell pepper, and onion on the baking sheet and drizzle the vegetables with the olive oil. Toss to coat the vegetables and spread them on the sheet in a single layer.

4. Roast in the oven until tender and lightly charred, about 20 minutes.

5. While the vegetables are roasting, bring the broth to a boil in a medium saucepan over high heat.

6. Remove the broth from the heat and stir in the couscous and raisins. Cover and set aside for 5 minutes.

7. Transfer the couscous to a large bowl and fluff with a fork. Stir in the dressing, roasted vegetables, almonds, and mint until well mixed.

8. Serve.

VARIATION TIP: There are many types of couscous used in Middle Eastern cooking, including peppercorn-size Israeli couscous, pea-size Lebanese couscous, and small instant couscous that is pre-steamed and dried. Follow the package instructions for the best results.

Mujadarra

SERVES 4 ♦ **PREP TIME:** 10 minutes ♦ **COOK TIME:** 60 minutes

This recipe attempts to follow the more traditional recipe by using lentils, brown rice, and a generous amount of olive oil to create richness in flavor. I didn't specify the lentils because I prefer the red ones, but green is the classic choice, so use whatever you have in your pantry.

¼ cup olive oil, divided

2 sweet onions, chopped

3 cups water or broth

1 cup lentils, rinsed

1 cup brown rice

½ teaspoon sea salt

1 sweet onion, thinly sliced

1. Heat 2 tablespoons of oil in a large saucepan over medium-high heat and sauté the chopped onion until lightly caramelized, stirring frequently, about 10 minutes.

2. Stir in the water, lentils, rice, and salt and bring to a boil. Reduce the heat to low and simmer, covered, until the lentils and rice are tender, about 45 minutes.

3. Remove the saucepan from the heat and let stand for 10 minutes.

4. Heat the remaining 2 tablespoons of oil in a medium skillet over medium-high heat and add the sliced onion. Sauté, stirring frequently until lightly caramelized, about 10 minutes.

5. Serve the lentils and rice topped with the sliced onion.

VARIATION TIP: In Lebanon, this dish is served both pureed and with the legumes and grain intact. A yogurt topping joins the onion. In Israel, the rice is sometimes swapped with bulgur and served with a salad.

Tabbouleh

SERVES 4 ♦ **PREP TIME:** 20 minutes ♦ **COOK TIME:** 20 minutes

Cold salads are a staple in my house, with Tabbouleh, a Lebanese national dish, at the top of the list of family favorites. I can whip this dish together in very little time because the ingredients are usually in my refrigerator—tomatoes, cucumber, parsley, lemons, and garlic. Cooking the bulgur takes the most time, but it can be prepared ahead and stored in a container to be used for this dish and for other recipes.

1 cup uncooked bulgur, rinsed and drained

2 cups boiling water

3 tablespoons olive oil

Juice of 1 lemon

1 teaspoon minced garlic

3 large tomatoes, chopped

2 scallions, white and green parts, finely chopped

1 English cucumber, diced

1 cup finely chopped fresh parsley

¼ cup finely chopped fresh mint

1. Put the bulgur in a large bowl and add the hot water.

2. Soak for 15 to 20 minutes or until tender, then drain the remaining water out of the bowl.

3. In a large bowl, whisk together the olive oil, lemon juice, and garlic. Stir in the bulgur, tomatoes, scallions, cucumber, parsley, and mint and stir to thoroughly combine.

4. Serve.

FUN FACT: Israel broke the Guinness World Record in 2009 for the largest bowl of Tabbouleh. It took more than 10 hours for 350 people to create a 9,532-pound, 12-ounce bowl that was more than 16 feet in diameter.

Turkish Baked Potato (Kumpir)

SERVES 4 ♦ **PREP TIME:** 20 minutes ♦ **COOK TIME:** 55 minutes

Kumpir is considered fast food in Turkey, where it is featured in cafés and street stands with heaps of toppings to suit any taste. Although not a traditional preparation, you can try this dish with sweet potatoes, as well.

4 large russet potatoes, scrubbed and pricked with a fork
1 tablespoon olive oil
Sea salt

Freshly ground black pepper
1 tablespoon butter, divided
1 cup shredded mozzarella cheese

Toppings (sliced black olives, pickled vegetables, cooked chicken or lamb, corn, other cheeses)

1. Preheat the oven to 400°F.

2. Line a small baking sheet with parchment paper and set aside.

3. Rub the potatoes all over with olive oil and season with salt and pepper. Place them on the baking sheet.

4. Bake until they are tender and the skins golden and crispy, 40 to 45 minutes.

5. Remove the potatoes from the oven and let stand for 10 minutes.

6. Cut the potato skins in half lengthwise to open a slit in the top, leaving the rest of the skin intact.

7. Spread the potatoes open and add butter, mashing it in gently with a fork to fluff up the flesh.

8. Divide the cheese among the potatoes, mixing it in gradually until the flesh is very soft.

9. Top the potatoes with your favorite toppings and serve.

VARIATION TIP: There is no limit to the toppings you can stuff into these fluffy potatoes, including vegan or vegetarian options. This makes them the perfect choice for large groups with lots of dietary considerations.

Fattoush

SERVES 4 ♦ **PREP TIME:** 30 minutes ♦ **COOK TIME:** 3 minutes

People who eat lots of freshly baked bread, like those in Italy and the Levant,
need ways to use it up when it gets stale. Salads are an excellent solution.

For the dressing

½ cup olive oil

Juice and zest of 2 lemons

1 teaspoon ground
  sumac (optional)

¼ teaspoon ground
  cinnamon

Sea salt

Freshly ground
  black pepper

For the salad

1 tablespoon olive oil

1 pita bread, cut into
  ½-inch pieces

½ teaspoon lemon-pepper
  seasoning or sumac

4 tomatoes, diced

4 cups chopped
  romaine lettuce

4 large radishes, chopped

1 English cucumber, diced

¼ sweet onion, chopped

1 cup chopped fresh parsley

½ cup chopped fresh mint

To make the dressing

In a small bowl, whisk together the olive oil, lemon juice, lemon zest, sumac
(if using), and cinnamon until well blended. Season to taste and set aside.

To make the salad

1. Heat the oil in a small skillet over medium-high heat.

2. Add the pita and sauté, stirring frequently, until golden and crispy all over,
   about 3 minutes.

3. Season with lemon pepper and set aside.

4. Toss the remaining ingredients together in a large bowl. Add the dressing
   and toss to coat.

5. Add the toasted pita just before serving, tossing to mix, and serve.

COOKING TIP: The baked pita can be made ahead and stored in a container at room temperature for up to 3 days. You can also bake the pita after tossing it in oil, in a 350°F oven for
10 minutes.

Turkish Bulgur Salad (Kisir)

SERVES 4 ♦ **PREP TIME:** 20 minutes ♦ **COOK TIME:** 15 minutes

Tomato paste might seem like an odd ingredient for a salad, but it is traditional in kisir. When added to honey and citrus, the taste really dances on the tongue, and the dressing tints the bulgur a pretty color.

1 cup bulgur

2 cups water or
  vegetable broth

3 tablespoons olive oil

2 tablespoons tomato paste

1 tablespoon honey

Juice and zest of ½ lemon

1 English cucumber,
  chopped

2 large tomatoes, chopped

3 tablespoons chopped
  fresh parsley

Sea salt, for seasoning

1. Pour the bulgur and water into a medium saucepan and bring to a boil over high heat.

2. Reduce the heat to low and simmer until the bulgur is tender, 12 to 15 minutes. Drain any excess liquid and allow the bulgur to cool to room temperature.

3. When the bulgur is cool, in a medium bowl, whisk together the olive oil, tomato paste, honey, lemon juice, and lemon zest.

4. Add the bulgur, cucumber, tomato, and parsley to the oil mixture and toss to combine.

5. Season with salt and serve.

MENU TIP: Serve this hearty, colorful salad with Fish Harrah (page 100), Middle Eastern Lamb Kebabs (page 105), or Spiced Beef Sausage (Merguez) (page 113) for a full, satisfying meal.

Rice Mejadra

SERVES 4 ♦ **PREP TIME:** 10 minutes ♦ **COOK TIME:** 50 minutes

This simple dish is similar to the ubiquitous red beans and rice in the southern United States, except this version uses a different legume. The combination of rice and beans creates a complete protein and is a natural pairing of the staple foods eaten all over the world, such as in Latin America, Africa, and the Middle East.

1 tablespoon olive oil	1 cup white rice	Juice of 1 lemon
1 sweet onion, chopped	1 cup lentils, rinsed	Sea salt
1 teaspoon minced garlic	3 cups water or broth	

1. Heat the oil in a large saucepan over medium-high heat.

2. Sauté the onion and garlic until lightly caramelized, stirring frequently, about 10 minutes.

3. Stir in the rice, lentils, and water, and bring the mixture to a boil.

4. Reduce the heat to low and simmer, partially covered, until the rice and lentils are tender, about 40 minutes.

5. Remove the saucepan from the heat, stir in the lemon juice, and season with salt.

6. Serve.

COOKING TIP: If you don't have time to sauté onions but still want to enjoy the crispy, sweet taste, try using a store-bought fried onion product. This is certainly untraditional and not as delicious as homemade, but it's very convenient.

Garlicky Lentil Salad (Salata Adas)

SERVES 4 ♦ **PREP TIME:** 20 minutes ♦ **COOK TIME:** 6 minutes

This salad features strong garlic flavor, olive oil, citrus, and heaps of fresh herbs. The colors are generally green from the lentils, parsley, and mint, but don't let this monochromatic presentation fool you; the flavors are exciting. Although not the usual serving style, I love tucking a couple of scoops of garlicky lentils into a pita for a quick lunch.

¼ cup olive oil, divided
1 tablespoon minced garlic
Juice of 1 lemon
2 tablespoons finely
   chopped fresh parsley
2 tablespoons chopped
   fresh mint

1 teaspoon ground cumin
Pinch allspice
1 (15-ounce) can
   sodium-free green lentils,
   drained and rinsed

Sea salt
Freshly ground
   black pepper

1. Heat 2 tablespoons of oil in a medium skillet over medium-high heat.

2. Sauté the garlic until it is lightly caramelized, stirring frequently, 5 to 6 minutes.

3. Remove the skillet from the heat and add the remaining 2 tablespoons of oil, the lemon juice, parsley, mint, cumin, and allspice, and stir to combine.

4. Stir in the lentils and season with salt and pepper.

5. Transfer the salad to a serving bowl and let it come to room temperature before serving.

COOKING TIP: Try adding pureed roasted garlic during step 3 to create a new flavor profile that is mellow and almost sweet.

Shirazi Salad

SERVES 4 ♦ **PREP TIME:** 20 minutes

This traditional Iranian salad is easy to make but packs lovely fresh-vegetable flavors into a simple preparation. The lime and olive oil dressing is ideal for a summer meal, especially if your tomatoes are ripe and still warm from the sun.

¼ cup olive oil

Juice of 1 lime

Sea salt

Freshly ground
   black pepper

4 English cucumbers, diced

3 tomatoes, seeded
   and diced

1 red onion, chopped

⅓ cup finely chopped
   fresh parsley

1. In a large bowl, whisk together the olive oil and lime juice, and season lightly with salt and pepper.

2. Stir in the cucumber, tomato, onion, and parsley and toss to combine.

3. Serve.

VARIATION TIP: If you can find it, the traditional dressing ingredient for this salad is verjuice, pressed juice of unripe grapes or other sour fruit, instead of lime juice.

Skillet Potatoes (Batata Harra)

SERVES 4 ♦ **PREP TIME:** 25 minutes ♦ **COOK TIME:** 25 minutes

These Lebanese-style potatoes might look like plain hash browns, but the first bite with its kick of spices, herbs, and tart lemon will take you to unexpected culinary heights. The trick to perfect potatoes that are crispy on the outside and tender on the inside is double processing them. By boiling them first, you remove some of the surface starch, which allows for a golden, unburned crust and a fluffy interior.

8 russet potatoes, peeled and quartered

¼ cup olive oil

1 tablespoon minced garlic

1 teaspoon ground coriander

1 teaspoon ground turmeric

½ teaspoon ground cumin

Juice of 1 lime

1 cup chopped fresh parsley

½ cup chopped fresh cilantro

¼ cup chopped fresh dill

Sea salt

Freshly ground black pepper

1. Put the potatoes in a large pot and cover them with about 2 inches of water.

2. Place the pot on high heat and bring it to a boil, cooking the potatoes until tender but still firm, about 15 minutes.

3. Drain the potatoes on paper towels until they're cool enough to touch. Cut the potatoes into 1-inch pieces and set aside.

4. Heat the olive oil in a large skillet over medium-high heat. Sauté the garlic until softened, about 3 minutes.

5. Stir in the coriander, turmeric, and cumin and sauté for 2 minutes.

6. Stir in the lime juice and potatoes and sauté for 5 minutes.

7. Remove the skillet from the heat and stir in the parsley, cilantro, and dill and season with salt and pepper.

8. Serve warm or at room temperature.

COOKING TIP: You can parboil the potatoes the day before and store them in the refrigerator in a sealed container. When sautéing the potatoes, add an extra 10 to 15 minutes to take them from chilled to hot.

Lebanese Rice

SERVES 4 ♦ **PREP TIME:** 10 minutes ♦ **COOK TIME:** 37 minutes

This might look like plain rice, but the sautéed noodles add an interesting texture and visual impact to the dish. Cooking the noodles dry means they develop a toasted flavor and retain a slightly chewy texture when simmered with the rice. Delicious!

1 tablespoon olive oil

½ cup vermicelli pasta

1 cup white rice, rinsed

Pinch allspice

2¼ cups water or
vegetable broth

Sea salt

1 tablespoon chopped
fresh parsley, for garnish

1. Heat the oil in a medium saucepan over medium heat and sauté the dry pasta until it is browned, stirring frequently, about 10 minutes.

2. Stir in the rice and allspice and sauté for 2 minutes.

3. Stir in the water and bring the mixture to a boil. Reduce the heat to low, cover, and cook until the rice is cooked through, about 25 minutes.

4. Season the mixture with salt and serve topped with parsley.

COOKING TIP: The vermicelli is sautéed instead of being cooked in water, so it creates an interesting texture and adds flecks of golden color to the white rice. The vermicelli softens when cooked, so don't worry—it won't be hard and unpalatable.

Middle Eastern Roasted Carrot Salad

SERVES 4 ♦ **PREP TIME:** 15 minutes ♦ **COOK TIME:** 40 minutes

Culinary magic happens when you toss carrots in oil and roast until tender. The carrots become mouthwateringly sweet, slightly crispy, and slightly smoky in flavor. When you add warm spices, citrus, and fresh herbs, simple carrots can become a meal.

8 carrots, cut into 1-inch chunks

2 tablespoons olive oil

Juice of 1 lemon

2 teaspoons minced garlic

1 teaspoon peeled and grated fresh ginger

1 teaspoon ground coriander

½ teaspoon ground cumin

¼ teaspoon ground cinnamon

⅛ teaspoon red pepper flakes

Pinch ground cloves

Sea salt

½ cup plain Greek yogurt

1 teaspoon chopped fresh dill, for garnish

1. Preheat the oven to 400°F.

2. Line a small baking sheet with parchment paper and set aside.

3. In a medium bowl, toss together the carrots, olive oil, lemon juice, garlic, ginger, coriander, cumin, cinnamon, red pepper flakes, and cloves.

4. Season lightly with salt and spread the vegetables on the baking sheet in a single layer.

5. Roast, turning once, until the carrots are tender and lightly caramelized, 35 to 40 minutes.

6. Transfer the carrots to a serving bowl and drizzle with the yogurt.

7. Serve topped with dill.

VARIATION TIP: Purple carrots are highest in antioxidants, so try this variety if it is available.

Israeli Couscous

SERVES 4 ♦ **PREP TIME:** 15 minutes ♦ **COOK TIME:** 12 minutes

If I had to pick a favorite couscous, I would take Israeli couscous every single time. The pearl-size balls and colorful chopped vegetables create a lovely mosaic in which every single ingredient shows up in each bite of the mixture.

1 teaspoon plus
  3 tablespoons
  olive oil, divided
1 cup pearl couscous
1¼ cups water

Juice and zest of ¼ orange
1 tablespoon freshly
  squeezed lemon juice
Sea salt, for seasoning
½ cup dried cranberries

¼ cup chopped pistachios
1 tablespoon chopped,
  fresh basil

1. Heat one teaspoon of the olive oil in a medium saucepan over medium-high heat.

2. Toast the couscous in the oil until lightly golden, about 2 minutes.

3. Add the water and bring the mixture to a boil. Reduce the heat to low and simmer until the liquid is absorbed, about 10 minutes.

4. In a medium bowl, whisk together the remaining 3 tablespoons of olive oil, the orange juice, orange zest, and lemon juice and season with salt.

5. Stir in the cooked couscous, cranberries, and pistachios.

6. Serve topped with basil.

FUN FACT: In Israel, the crack of a pistachio shell is considered to be good luck, especially for relationships.

Arnabeet

SERVES 4 ♦ **PREP TIME:** 15 minutes ♦ **COOK TIME:** 15 minutes

Although this dish does not have the healthiest preparation, you might be sur-prised to find that the finished vegetable pieces are not greasy. In fact, they are lightly caramelized due to the step requiring you to blot the cauliflower on paper towels. This dish is served with tahini sauce, but you can also try it with a creamy garlic yogurt sauce or a drizzle of Harissa (page 148).

Vegetable oil or ghee,
  for deep-frying
1 large head cauliflower, cut
  into small florets

Juice of 1 lemon
Sea salt
½ cup Tahini Sauce
  (page 142)

1 tablespoon chopped fresh
  cilantro, for garnish

1. Heat about 3 inches of oil in a medium deep skillet until it is 350°F.

2. Fry the cauliflower in batches until it is golden brown and tender, about 5 minutes per batch.

3. Transfer the fried cauliflower to a paper-towel-lined plate and blot to remove any excess oil.

4. Put the fried cauliflower in a serving bowl, toss with the lemon juice, and season with salt.

5. Drizzle the cauliflower with the tahini sauce.

6. Serve garnished with cilantro.

VARIATION TIP: If you want an Israeli version, serve with a strained yogurt or Schug (page 144). This recipe can be stuffed into a pita or served as a side dish.

Harissa-Roasted Cauliflower

SERVES 4 ♦ **PREP TIME:** 15 minutes ♦ **COOK TIME:** 30 minutes

Roasting cauliflower is one of the easiest ways to create a fabulous side dish with almost no effort at all. Cauliflower can be challenging to cook because it gets too soft very quickly if blanched too long. Roasting it ensures a tender, lightly cara-melized result every time, with no unpleasant mushy texture.

1 large cauliflower, cut into 1-inch slices with the core intact

2 tablespoons homemade Harissa (page 148) or store-bought

1 tablespoon olive oil

½ cup crumbled goat cheese

¼ cup chopped fresh parsley

1. Preheat the oven to 400°F.
2. Line a baking sheet with parchment paper and arrange the cauliflower slices on it in a single layer with no overlap.
3. Brush the cauliflower slices with the harissa and drizzle with the olive oil.
4. Roast the cauliflower until it is tender, 25 to 30 minutes.
5. Arrange the roasted cauliflower on a serving plate and sprinkle with goat cheese and parsley.
6. Serve.

COOKING TIP: As an alternative to slicing the cauliflower, spread the harissa all over the cauli-flower head, put it in a Dutch oven with the lid on, and bake in the oven for 40 to 50 minutes.

Persian Stew
with Walnuts
and Pomegranate
(Fesenjan), page 74

Chapter Four

SOUPS AND STEWS

Soups and stews with accompanying grains or legumes are often eaten at a communal table with one large platter of food in the middle. The food is either spooned onto individual plates or scooped directly from the dish with pita, utensils, or fingers, depending on the country or occasion. I have fond memories of many hearty, flavorful stews and of fluffy couscous enjoyed with companions engaging in lively conversation.

Lebanese Beef Stew (Bazella Riz Lahme)

SERVES 4 ♦ **PREP TIME:** 20 minutes ♦ **COOK TIME:** 2 hours and 21 minutes

You will think you are looking at a classic beef stew filled with onions, beef chunks, and pretty green peas until you catch a whiff of the complex warm spices in this dish. Cinnamon, cloves, and lemony cardamom waft off the steaming stew and call out for a good slice of bread to soak up every last drop of sauce.

3 tablespoons olive oil

2 pounds cubed
  stewing beef

2 sweet onions, chopped

3 teaspoons minced garlic

¼ cup tomato paste

4 cups low-sodium
  beef broth

4 bay leaves

1 teaspoon ground
  cinnamon

1 teaspoon ground
  cardamom

½ teaspoon ground allspice

¼ teaspoon ground cloves

2 cups frozen or fresh
  green peas

Sea salt

Freshly ground
  black pepper

1 tablespoon chopped
  fresh parsley

1. Heat the oil in a large skillet over medium-high heat and brown the beef, stirring frequently, about 5 minutes. Remove the beef to a plate, using a slotted spoon, and set aside.

2. Add the onions and garlic to the skillet and sauté until softened, about 3 minutes.

3. Stir in the tomato paste and cook for 3 minutes, scraping up any cooked bits. Add the beef broth, bay leaves, cinnamon, cardamom, allspice, and cloves and stir to combine.

4. Add the beef back to the skillet and bring the liquid to a boil. Cover and reduce the heat to low, and simmer, stirring occasionally, until the beef is tender, 1½ to 2 hours.

5. Remove the bay leaves and stir in the peas.

6. Simmer 10 minutes more and season with salt and pepper.

7. Serve topped with parsley.

COOKING TIP: This recipe can also be made in a slow cooker. Brown the beef in a skillet and then add the beef and the other ingredients (except salt, pepper, and parsley) to the slow cooker. Heat on low for 8 to 9 hours, season with salt and pepper, and serve topped with parsley.

Persian Herb Stew (Ghormeh Sabzi)

SERVES 4 ♦ **PREP TIME:** 20 minutes ♦ **COOK TIME:** 2 hours and 35 minutes

Ghormeh sabzi is an Iranian national dish featuring heaps of fresh herbs and scallions. If you want to create a southern Iranian version, stir in ¼ cup of tomato paste with the broth. Or try the southwestern version popular in Fars province by adding diced potatoes to the stew. Whichever variation you make, the stew will be appealing.

3 tablespoons olive oil, divided

1 pound boneless lamb, cubed

1 sweet onion, chopped

2 teaspoons minced garlic

1 teaspoon ground turmeric

3 cups low-sodium beef broth

3 scallions, green parts only, chopped

1 cup chopped fresh parsley

½ cup chopped spinach

¼ cup chopped fresh cilantro

1 (15-ounce) can low-sodium kidney beans, drained and rinsed

2 tablespoons dried fenugreek

Sea salt

Freshly ground black pepper

Juice and zest of 2 limes

1. Heat 1 tablespoon of oil in a large stockpot over medium-high heat.

2. Sauté the lamb until it is browned on all sides and cooked halfway through, about 15 minutes.

3. Remove the lamb to a plate using a slotted spoon and set aside.

4. Add 1 tablespoon of the oil to the stockpot and sauté the onion, garlic, and turmeric until softened, about 5 minutes.

5. Return the lamb to the stockpot and add the broth. Bring to a boil, reduce the heat to low, partially cover, and simmer for 1 hour.

6. While the lamb is simmering, heat the remaining 1 tablespoon of oil in a medium skillet over medium heat.

7. Sauté the scallions, parsley, spinach, and cilantro until fragrant and wilted, about 20 minutes.

CONTINUED ▶

8. Stir the wilted herbs, beans, and fenugreek into the stew and continue simmering until the lamb is very tender, 1 hour to 1¼ hours more.

9. Season with salt and pepper and stir in the lime juice and lime zest.

10. Serve.

COOKING TIP: This recipe uses lime zest and lime juice to add the signature citrus twist. However, the traditional ingredient is Limu Omani or Persian limes that have been dried in the sun for weeks. You can find this ingredient in some specialty markets or online.

Middle Eastern Lamb Stew

SERVES 4 ♦ **PREP TIME:** 20 minutes ♦ **COOK TIME:** 2 hours and 30 minutes

I combined some of my favorite Middle Eastern ingredients in this stew, such as heaps of spices, tender lamb, and, of course, chickpeas. The finished meal is ideal for blustery winter nights when you need to be warmed from the inside.

3 tablespoons olive oil, divided

1 pound boneless lamb shoulder meat, cut into 1-inch chunks

1 sweet onion, chopped

1 tablespoon minced garlic

1 tablespoon ground cumin

2 teaspoons ground coriander

¼ teaspoon chili powder

1 (28-ounce) can diced tomatoes

2 cups low-sodium beef broth

1 (15-ounce) can low-sodium chickpeas, drained and rinsed

8 ounces Swiss chard, chopped

Sea salt

Freshly ground black pepper

1. Heat 2 tablespoons of oil in a large stockpot over medium-high heat.

2. Sauté the lamb until it is browned on all sides and cooked halfway through, about 15 minutes.

3. Remove the lamb to a plate using a slotted spoon and set aside.

4. Add the remaining 2 tablespoons of oil to the stockpot and sauté the onion, garlic, cumin, coriander, and chili powder until softened and very fragrant, about 5 minutes.

5. Return the lamb to the pot and stir in the tomatoes and broth. Bring the stew to a boil, reduce the heat to low, partially cover, and simmer until the meat is very tender, about 2 hours.

6. Stir in the chickpeas and Swiss chard and simmer until the greens are wilted and the chickpeas are heated through, about 10 minutes.

7. Season with salt and pepper.

8. Serve.

COOKING TIP: Store any remaining Swiss chard, unwashed, in a bag with the air pressed out in the refrigerator for up to 1 week.

Green Bean and Beef Stew (Fasulia)

SERVES 4 ♦ **PREP TIME:** 20 minutes ♦ **COOK TIME:** 2 hours and 26 minutes

This dish shows its true beauty at your first bite of the spiced, full-bodied sauce and filling beef chunks. This classic Egyptian stew might become your new favorite.

3 tablespoons olive oil, divided

1 pound cubed stewing beef

1 sweet onion, chopped

1 tablespoon minced garlic

½ cup tomato paste

4 cups low-sodium beef broth

1 (15-ounce) can low-sodium crushed tomatoes

1 teaspoon ground coriander

1 teaspoon ground cumin

¼ teaspoon ground allspice

1 pound green beans, trimmed and cut into 1-inch pieces

Sea salt

Freshly ground black pepper

1 tablespoon chopped fresh parsley, for garnish

1. Heat 2 tablespoons of oil in a large stockpot over medium-high heat.

2. Sauté the beef until it is browned on all sides and cooked halfway through, about 15 minutes.

3. Remove the beef to a plate using a slotted spoon and set aside.

4. Add the remaining 2 tablespoons of oil to the stockpot and sauté the onion and garlic until softened, about 3 minutes.

5. Stir in the tomato paste and sauté 3 minutes.

6. Return the beef to the pot and stir in the broth, tomatoes, coriander, cumin, and allspice.

7. Bring the stew to a boil, reduce the heat to low, partially cover, and simmer until the meat is very tender, 1½ to 2 hours.

8. Stir in the green beans and simmer until they are tender, about 5 minutes.

9. Season the stew with salt and pepper, and serve, garnished with parsley.

COOKING TIP: To make the stew in an oven, brown the meat in an oven-safe casserole dish and stir in the remaining ingredients (except the beans, salt, pepper, and parsley). Bake at 375°F, covered, until the meat is very tender, about 1½ hours. Then stir in the beans, season with salt and pepper, and serve garnished with parsley.

Mulukhiyah

SERVES 4 ♦ **PREP TIME:** 10 minutes ♦ **COOK TIME:** 19 minutes

This soup is a national dish of Egypt but is also very popular in Syria, Palestine, and Jordan. The traditional main ingredient, a bitter green called mulukhiyah (see tip), creates a thick, almost gelatinous texture similar to okra. You can add shredded chicken to the soup for extra protein and bulk.

2 tablespoons olive oil

½ sweet onion, chopped

1 tablespoon minced garlic

1 tablespoon ground coriander

1 tablespoon ground cumin

5 cups low-sodium vegetable or chicken broth

1 pound fresh baby spinach or mulukhiyah

Juice of 2 lemons

Sea salt

Freshly ground black pepper

2 cups cooked rice

1. Heat the oil in a large saucepan over medium-high heat.

2. Sauté the onion and garlic until tender, about 3 minutes.

3. Stir in the coriander and cumin and sauté 1 minute more.

4. Add the broth and spinach and bring to a boil.

5. Reduce the heat to low and simmer until the spinach is very tender, about 15 minutes.

6. Stir in the lemon juice and season with salt and pepper.

7. Serve the soup spooned over the cooked rice.

COOKING TIP: Mulukhiyah (also known as Egyptian spinach, Jew's mallow, and jute leaf) is a bitter green that is popular in many Middle Eastern countries. Spinach is an acceptable substitution in this version of the recipe.

Red Lentil Soup (Shorbat Adas)

SERVES 4 ♦ **PREP TIME:** 20 minutes ♦ **COOK TIME:** 41 minutes

I like my lentil soup very thick and porridge-like, rather than being able to see individual legumes, so the cooking time is a bit longer. If you like a "firmer" soup, stop simmering when the lentils are just tender, or use green lentils, which retain their shape better than red.

2 tablespoons olive oil
1 sweet onion, chopped
1 tablespoon minced garlic
2 celery stalks, chopped
2 carrots, chopped
6 cups low-sodium
  vegetable broth

2 cups red lentils, rinsed
  and picked over
1 (15-ounce) can
  low-sodium
  diced tomatoes
2 teaspoons ground cumin
½ teaspoon paprika

½ teaspoon turmeric
2 cups fresh baby spinach
Sea salt
Freshly ground
  black pepper

1. Heat the oil in a large stockpot over medium-high heat.
2. Sauté the onion and garlic until softened, about 3 minutes.
3. Stir in the celery and carrots and sauté for 5 minutes, stirring frequently.
4. Stir in the broth, lentils, tomatoes, cumin, paprika, and turmeric and bring the soup to a boil.
5. Reduce the heat to low and simmer until the lentils and vegetables are very tender, 25 to 30 minutes.
6. Stir in the spinach and simmer 3 minutes more to wilt the greens.
7. Season with salt and pepper and serve.

MENU TIP: Serve this hearty soup with Shirazi Salad (page 51) or Fattoush (page 47) to create a well-rounded dinner.

Turkish White Beans (Kuru Fasulye)

SERVES 4 ♦ **PREP TIME:** 15 minutes, plus soaking time
♦ **COOK TIME:** 2 hours and 34 minutes

Kuru Fasulye means "dried beans," which is apropos because they are the main ingredient of this popular comfort food. Many recipes add beef or lamb to the pot, but this vegetarian meal is just as satisfying. You can use canned white beans, but you will lose some of the flavors because dried beans soak up everything while they cook.

2 cups dried white beans, rinsed and picked through

2 tablespoons olive oil

2 celery stalks, chopped

1 sweet onion, chopped

1 teaspoon minced garlic

1 (15-ounce) can crushed tomatoes

2 tablespoons tomato paste

1 tablespoon homemade Harissa (page 148) or store-bought

1 cup water

Sea salt

Freshly ground black pepper

1. Put the beans in a medium bowl and cover them with about 2 inches of water. Soak overnight or longer. Just before cooking, drain the beans and rinse them in cold water.

2. Put the beans in a medium saucepan and cover with about 2 inches of water. Place the beans on high heat and bring to a boil. Reduce the heat to low and simmer, partially covered, until the beans are tender, stirring occasionally, 1 to 1½ hours. Drain the beans and return them to the saucepan.

3. While the beans are cooking, heat the oil in a small skillet over medium-high heat and sauté the celery, onion, and garlic until softened, about 3 minutes.

4. Stir in the tomatoes, tomato paste, and harissa and sauté 1 minute more. Remove the skillet from the heat.

5. Add the tomato sauce to the drained, cooked beans along with 1 cup of water.

6. Bring to a boil, reduce the heat to low, and simmer for 1 hour or until the sauce is thickened.

7. Season with salt and pepper and serve.

VARIATION TIP: Sausage, lamb, or beef can be added to this bean-based dish. This stew can be served over fluffy cooked rice or bulgur.

Kuwaiti Lamb Stew (Machboos Laham)

SERVES 4 ♦ **PREP TIME:** 20 minutes ♦ **COOK TIME:** 2 hours and 45 minutes

Machboos Laham is a Kuwaiti national dish and can feature different varieties of meat rather than lamb. The exciting part of this dish is that the flavorful rice cooks within the stew and still retains its texture rather than falling apart.

3 tablespoons olive
 oil, divided

1 pound boneless lamb
 shoulder meat, cut into
 1-inch chunks

1 sweet onion, chopped

1 tablespoon minced garlic

1 tablespoon Middle
 Eastern Spice Blend
 (Bahārāt) (page 147)

1 teaspoon ground
 cardamom

1 teaspoon turmeric

½ teaspoon ground cloves

6 cups low-sodium
 chicken broth

1 (15-ounce) can
 low-sodium diced
 tomatoes

1 cup long-grain rice

Juice and zest of 1 lime

Sea salt

Freshly ground
 black pepper

½ cup chopped fresh
 cilantro, for garnish

1. Heat 2 tablespoons of oil in a large stockpot over medium-high heat.

2. Sauté the lamb until it is browned on all sides and cooked halfway through, about 15 minutes.

3. Remove the lamb to a plate using a slotted spoon and set aside.

4. Add the remaining 1 tablespoon of oil to the stockpot and sauté the onion and garlic until softened, about 3 minutes.

5. Stir in the Bahārāt, cardamom, turmeric, and cloves and sauté for 1 minute.

6. Return the lamb to the pot and stir in the broth and tomatoes.

7. Bring the stew to a boil, reduce the heat to low, partially cover, and simmer until the meat is very tender, 1½ to 2 hours.

8. Stir in the rice, lime juice, and lime zest, and simmer until the rice is cooked, about 25 minutes.

9. Season with salt and pepper and serve topped with cilantro.

VARIATION TIP: If you want to create the Bahrain version, use chicken instead of lamb and add extra lime juice and zest to replace the traditional dried limes.

Vegetable Harira Soup

SERVES 4 ♦ **PREP TIME:** 20 minutes ♦ **COOK TIME:** 42 minutes

I came in a tad late one day to my kitchen in Tripoli, and my Moroccan sous chef was already busy at the stove, making something that smelled absolutely heavenly. This is now my go-to soup when I need a lift in spirits or feel slightly under the weather. Thank you, Abdullah!

2 tablespoons olive oil

2 celery stalks, chopped

1 large carrot, chopped

1 cup chopped mushrooms

½ sweet onion, chopped

1 tablespoon minced garlic

1 (15-ounce) can low-sodium diced tomatoes

2 tablespoons tomato paste

2 teaspoons ground cumin

1 teaspoon smoked paprika

½ teaspoon ground cinnamon

¼ teaspoon chili powder

4 cups low-sodium vegetable broth

1 cup cooked chickpeas

1 cup cooked lentils

Juice of 1 lemon

Sea salt

2 tablespoons chopped fresh parsley, for garnish

1. Heat the oil in a large stockpot over medium heat.

2. Sauté the celery, carrot, mushrooms, onion, and garlic, stirring frequently, until the vegetables are softened, about 10 minutes.

3. Stir in the tomatoes, tomato paste, cumin, paprika, cinnamon, and chili powder and sauté for 2 minutes.

4. Stir in the broth, chickpeas, and lentils and bring the soup to a boil. Reduce the heat to low and simmer until the legumes and vegetables are very tender, about 30 minutes.

5. Stir in the lemon juice and season with salt.

6. Serve topped with parsley.

VARIATION TIP: Traditional Moroccan harira soup often contains vermicelli pasta along with the legumes, so try adding 1 cup vermicelli about 10 minutes before the end of the cooking time.

Moroccan Chicken Noodle Soup (Chicken Chorba)

SERVES 4 ♦ **PREP TIME:** 20 minutes ♦ **COOK TIME:** 35 minutes

Chicken soup is a basic need, ideal for when you are sick or need a healthy, light meal at the end of a busy day. Chicken Chorba is made with simple cooking techniques and unprocessed ingredients, so you can duplicate this recipe no matter where you are in the world.

1 tablespoon olive oil
2 celery stalks, chopped
1 sweet onion, chopped
2 teaspoons peeled and grated fresh ginger
¼ cup tomato paste
2 teaspoons turmeric

6 cups low-sodium chicken broth
4 cups chopped, cooked chicken
3 carrots, diced
2 potatoes, diced
½ cup vermicelli noodles, broken into 2-inch pieces

Juice of 1 lime
1 tablespoon chopped fresh parsley
1 tablespoon chopped fresh cilantro
Sea salt

1. Heat the oil in a large stockpot over medium-high heat.
2. Sauté the celery, onion, and ginger until softened, about 4 minutes.
3. Stir in the tomato paste and turmeric and sauté 1 minute more.
4. Stir in the broth, chicken, carrots, and potatoes and bring the soup to a boil.
5. Reduce the heat to low and simmer until the vegetables are tender, about 20 minutes.
6. Add the vermicelli and simmer until the noodles are tender, about 10 minutes.
7. Stir in the lime juice, parsley, and cilantro, and season the soup with salt.
8. Serve.

COOKING TIP: You can use raw chicken in this soup for a traditional preparation. Simply chop the chicken and sauté it with the onion and garlic and simmer the chicken in the broth for at least 30 minutes before adding the remaining vegetables and finishing the recipe.

Freekeh Soup

SERVES 4 ♦ **PREP TIME:** 10 minutes, plus soaking time ♦ **COOK TIME:** 50 minutes

Look up the word potage, *and you will get a good idea what to expect when making freekeh soup: simmered grains, thick and almost mushy in texture. Freekeh is an ancient grain that is toasted, so the flavor is exceptional. You will find different variations of this tasty dish in Palestine, Jordan, Egypt, Lebanon, and Syria.*

1 cup freekeh

1 tablespoon olive oil

1 sweet onion, chopped

1 teaspoon minced garlic

2 teaspoons Middle Eastern Spice Blend (Bahārāt) (page 147)

5 cups vegetable or chicken broth

Sea salt

1 tablespoon chopped fresh parsley, for garnish

1. Put the freekeh in a medium bowl and cover it with about 2 inches of water. Set aside to soak overnight. Just before making the soup, drain the freekeh and rinse in cold water.

2. Heat the oil in a large saucepan over medium-high heat and sauté the onion and garlic until softened, about 3 minutes.

3. Stir in the Bahārāt and sauté 2 minutes more.

4. Stir in the broth and the rinsed freekeh and bring the soup to a boil. Reduce the heat to low and simmer until the grains are very tender and the soup is thickened, about 45 minutes.

5. Season with salt and serve topped with parsley.

VARIATION TIP: Shredded chicken is a common ingredient in this hearty soup. You can also top the dish with a spoonful of thick Greek yogurt for a lovely creamy finish.

Persian Creamy Barley Soup (Soup-e Jo)

SERVES 4 ♦ **PREP TIME:** 20 minutes ♦ **COOK TIME:** 56 minutes

In Middle Eastern recipes, barley is not usually the main ingredient, as it is in this Iranian creation. The texture is both slightly chewy from the grain and creamy due to a generous scoop of yogurt.

1 tablespoon olive oil

3 leeks, white and green parts, chopped

2 celery stalks, chopped

1 tablespoon minced garlic

1 teaspoon Ras El Hanout (page 151)

6 cups low-sodium vegetable broth

½ cup barley

2 carrots, diced

2 bay leaves

Juice of 1 lemon

½ cup Greek yogurt

Sea salt

Freshly ground black pepper

3 tablespoons chopped fresh cilantro

1. Heat the oil in a large stockpot over medium-high heat.

2. Sauté the leeks, celery, garlic, and Ras El Hanout until the vegetables are tender, about 6 minutes.

3. Stir in the broth, barley, carrots, and bay leaves and bring the soup to a boil.

4. Reduce the heat to low and simmer until the barley and vegetables are tender, about 50 minutes.

5. Remove the bay leaves and puree half the soup with an immersion blender (or in a food processor). Recombine the pureed portion with the other portion.

6. Stir in the lemon juice and yogurt and season the soup with salt and pepper.

7. Serve topped with cilantro.

VARIATION TIP: The traditional recipe relies on a bechamel sauce, rather than yogurt. A simple bechamel is 2 tablespoons each of flour and butter whisked over medium heat for 2 minutes in a medium saucepan. Then, 1 cup of milk is whisked in until the sauce is thick and smooth, about 5 minutes.

Lentil and Tomato Soup (Shawrbat 'Adas Maa Banadoura)

SERVES 4 ♦ **PREP TIME:** 20 minutes ♦ **COOK TIME:** 43 minutes

Lentils have been a main ingredient in Middle Eastern cooking for thousands of years. This citrus-spiked, tomato-based soup includes rice for even more healthy fiber and nutrients. Yellow or orange lentils would look lovely if you have them in your pantry.

1 tablespoon olive oil
1 sweet onion, chopped
1 tablespoon minced garlic
5 cups low-sodium
  vegetable broth
1 (15-ounce) can
  low-sodium stewed
  tomatoes

1 cup red lentils, picked over
  and rinsed
¼ cup long-grain rice
1 teaspoon cumin
1 teaspoon ground
  coriander
½ teaspoon paprika
Pinch red pepper flakes

Sea salt
Freshly ground
  black pepper
Juice of 1 lemon

1. Heat the oil in a large stockpot over medium-high heat.
2. Sauté the onion and garlic until the vegetables are tender, about 3 minutes.
3. Stir in the broth, tomatoes, lentils, rice, cumin, coriander, paprika, and red pepper flakes and bring the soup to a boil.
4. Reduce the heat to low and simmer until the lentils and rice are tender, about 40 minutes.
5. Season the soup with salt and pepper and stir in the lemon juice.
6. Serve.

MENU TIP: The rice in the soup breaks down and adds texture and taste while making the soup thick enough that it can be spooned over bulgur or couscous.

Persian Stew with Walnuts and Pomegranate (Fesenjan)

SERVES 4 ♦ **PREP TIME:** 20 minutes ♦ **COOK TIME:** 1 hour and 16 minutes

Toasty walnuts and tart pomegranate create a luscious sauce you might lick right out of the bowl. If you can find pomegranate molasses in a specialty market, it adds a lovely taste to the finished dish. You can create your own pomegranate molasses by simmering pure pomegranate juice until it is syrupy.

3 tablespoons olive oil, divided

1 pound boneless skinless chicken thighs, cut into 1-inch chunks

1 sweet onion, chopped

1 tablespoon minced garlic

1½ teaspoons ground cumin

½ teaspoon ground cinnamon

½ teaspoon ground nutmeg

¼ teaspoon turmeric

2 cups low-sodium chicken broth

1½ cups ground toasted walnuts

¼ cup pomegranate molasses or maple syrup

Juice and zest of 1 orange

Sea salt

Freshly ground black pepper

3 tablespoons chopped fresh parsley, for garnish

3 tablespoons pomegranate seeds, for garnish

1. Heat 2 tablespoons oil in a large stockpot over medium-high heat.

2. Sauté the chicken until it is browned on all sides, about 10 minutes.

3. Remove the chicken to a plate using a slotted spoon and set aside.

4. Add the remaining 1 tablespoon of oil to the stockpot and sauté the onion and garlic until softened, about 3 minutes.

5. Stir in the cumin, cinnamon, nutmeg, and turmeric and sauté 3 minutes.

6. Return the chicken to the pot and stir in the broth, walnuts, molasses, orange juice, and orange zest.

7. Bring the stew to a boil, reduce the heat to low, partially cover, and simmer until the chicken is very tender, about 1 hour.

8. Season the stew with salt and pepper.

9. Serve garnished with parsley and pomegranate seeds.

Persian Eggplant Soup (Ash-e Bademjan)

SERVES 4 ♦ **PREP TIME:** 20 minutes ♦ **COOK TIME:** 43 minutes

My father traveled and worked in many Middle Eastern countries and he often brought home handwritten recipes from various colleagues. This recipe was on one of those scraps of paper. As a child, I did not know the soup was made of eggplant. I just knew it was appealing and the crispy fried onion topping looked like a golden crown. I still arrange the onions in a perfect circle whenever I make this recipe.

2 tablespoons olive oil

1 sweet onion, chopped

1 tablespoon minced garlic

1 teaspoon turmeric

6 cups low-sodium vegetable broth

2 eggplants, peeled and cut into chunks

½ cup lentils, picked through and rinsed

1 (15-ounce) can low-sodium chickpeas, drained and rinsed

Sea salt

Freshly ground black pepper

1 cup kashk (see page 25), divided

½ cup Crispy Fried Onions (page 145)

1 tablespoon dried mint

1. Heat the oil in a large stockpot over medium-high heat.

2. Sauté the onion, garlic, and turmeric until the vegetables are tender, about 3 minutes.

3. Stir in the broth, eggplant, and lentils and bring the soup to a boil.

4. Reduce the heat to low and simmer for 20 minutes.

5. Stir in the chickpeas and simmer until the vegetables and lentils are tender, about 20 minutes.

6. Season the soup with salt and pepper.

7. Stir in ½ cup kashk.

8. Serve topped with a drizzle of the remaining kashk, crispy fried onions, and mint.

VARIATION TIP: This soup is vegetarian, but it can be made with lamb. If you need a vegan version of this thick soup, omit the kashk.

Turkish Poached
Eggs with Garlic
Yogurt (Cilbir),
page 80

Chapter Five

BREAKFAST

B reakfast in the Middle East is not typically what you might enjoy in Western countries; the dishes are robust and often include items one might associate with meals later in the day, such as hummus, olives, and beans. You will find eggs, oatmeal, and pancakes on the menu, but with slightly different preparation and flavor profiles. If you want to try a traditional Middle Eastern breakfast, make sure you include pita bread and a cup of tea. These recipes are flavorful, nourishing, and filling: a perfect start to a busy day.

Turkish Eggs (Menemen)

SERVES 4 ♦ **PREP TIME:** 20 minutes ♦ **COOK TIME:** 20 minutes

Menemen is found in cafés and restaurants in Turkey as a breakfast offering. Most of the recipes feature moist scrambled eggs mixed with tomatoes, hot peppers, onions, and herbs. The dish will not look like familiar Western-style eggs, yellow and fluffy, but rather more like a Southwest salsa and bean breakfast creation in which all the ingredients are mixed together.

2 tablespoons olive oil

1 sweet onion, chopped

1 hot pepper, chopped

1 tablespoon minced garlic

1 green bell pepper, finely chopped

1 red bell pepper, finely chopped

1 teaspoon chopped fresh oregano

½ teaspoon paprika

1 (15-ounce) can low-sodium diced tomatoes, drained

Sea salt

Freshly ground black pepper

8 large eggs, beaten

1 tablespoon chopped fresh mint, for garnish

1. Heat the oil in a large skillet over medium-high heat.

2. Sauté the onion, hot pepper, and garlic until softened, about 4 minutes.

3. Add the bell peppers, oregano, and paprika and sauté 6 minutes more.

4. Stir in the tomatoes and bring the sauce to a simmer, stirring until any purged liquid is evaporated, about 5 minutes. Season with salt and pepper.

5. Move the vegetables and tomatoes to one side of the skillet and pour in the beaten eggs. Scramble the eggs until just cooked through, forming large fluffy curds, mixing the vegetables into the eggs as you scramble them, about 5 minutes.

6. Serve topped with mint.

MENU TIP: Serve this colorful dish with Pita Bread (page 22) or with a plate of fresh fruit as a delicious healthy breakfast.

Yemeni Banana Bread Pudding (Masoub)

SERVES 4 ♦ **PREP TIME:** 15 minutes ♦ **COOK TIME:** 5 minutes

Toasted pita bread crumbs and ripe banana blend together to form a creamy, rich base that is then topped with sweet honey and raisins, crunchy almonds, and decadent whipped cream. You might never eat oatmeal again!

2 pita breads
2 cups mashed ripe banana
½ cup golden raisins

½ cup toasted
  sliced almonds
¼ cup honey

½ cup whipped
  (heavy) cream

1. Preheat the oven to 350°F.

2. Place the pitas on a baking sheet and toast in the oven until very dry and crispy, turning once, about 5 minutes in total.

3. Remove the pitas from the oven and let cool for 10 minutes. Pulse them in a food processor or use a box grater to create crumbs. Use 2 cups of crumbs for this recipe and store the rest in a sealed container in the freezer for up to 1 month.

4. In a medium bowl, mix together the pita crumbs and mashed banana until well combined.

5. Transfer the banana mixture to four serving bowls and evenly divide the raisins, almonds, honey, and whipped cream among the bowls.

6. Serve.

VARIATION TIP: Instead of whipped cream, you can drizzle the dish with a little condensed milk.

Turkish Poached Eggs with Garlic Yogurt (Cilbir)

SERVES 4 ♦ **PREP TIME:** 10 minutes ♦ **COOK TIME:** 3 minutes

In my 25 years of working as a chef, I never put eggs and yogurt together in the same dish. The first time I saw it was when working with a Turkish sous chef who made his own breakfast after a long shift. I tried a bite and was immediately a convert to cilbir. *The tangy, garlicky yogurt and luscious egg yolk were a perfect pairing. All I needed was a little bread to wipe the plate clean.*

2 cups plain Greek yogurt	Freshly ground	4 large eggs
2 teaspoons minced garlic	black pepper	½ teaspoon red
Sea salt	1 tablespoon white vinegar	pepper flakes

1. In a small bowl, stir together the yogurt and garlic until well blended and season with salt and pepper.

2. Divide the yogurt among four plates, spooning it into the middle of each and spreading it out slightly with the back of the spoon. Set the plates aside.

3. Place a large saucepan with 3 to 4 inches of water and the vinegar in it over high heat and bring to a boil.

4. Reduce the heat to low so that the water gently simmers.

5. Crack an egg into a small bowl and gently slip the egg into the simmering water. Repeat with the other three eggs.

6. Poach the eggs for about 3 minutes until the whites are firm.

7. Remove the poached eggs using a slotted spoon and drain on paper towels.

8. Put the drained eggs on the garlic yogurt mixture and sprinkle with red pepper flakes to serve.

COOKING TIP: Fresh eggs work best when poaching because the whites are firmer, so they envelope the yolk better. You can poach the eggs ahead of time, cool them in an ice bath, and store them in a container in the refrigerator for up to 4 days. To use, put the cold poached egg in a bowl of hot water for about 40 seconds to warm it up.

Eggs in Tomato Sauce (Shakshuka)

SERVES 4 ♦ **PREP TIME:** 15 minutes ♦ **COOK TIME:** 15 minutes

What could be more delicious than eggs poached in a spicy tomato and hot pepper sauce? Shakshuka was a traditional recipe in Libya, and I never took it off my menu because the patrons loved it. The best part of preparing this recipe is that I could put together the tasty tomato sauce in advance and warm it in a skillet before adding the eggs. The sauce will keep in the refrigerator for up to 4 days.

¼ cup olive oil
½ onion, diced
2 jalapeño peppers, seeded and chopped
1 tablespoon minced garlic

1 (28-ounce) can low-sodium diced tomatoes
Juice from 1 lemon
2 teaspoons paprika

1 teaspoon ground cumin
8 large eggs
1 cup crumbled feta cheese
2 tablespoons chopped fresh parsley, for garnish

1. Heat the oil in a large skillet over medium-high heat.

2. Sauté the onion, jalapeños, and garlic until softened, about 4 minutes.

3. Stir in the tomatoes, lemon juice, paprika, and cumin and bring the mixture to a simmer.

4. Use the back of a spoon to make 8 wells in the tomato mixture, then crack an egg into each well. Cover the skillet with a lid and let cook until the egg whites are no longer translucent, 4 to 5 minutes.

5. Remove from the heat and serve topped with feta and parsley.

VARIATION TIP: The Tunisian version of this Middle Eastern dish can include potatoes or chopped artichoke hearts, along with the classic ingredients.

Fava Bean Stew (Ful Mudammas)

SERVES 4 ♦ **PREP TIME:** 10 minutes, plus soaking time ♦ **COOK TIME:** 55 minutes

This Egyptian staple food has its origins thousands of years ago when meat was a luxury and a steaming bowl of tender fava beans kept you going all day. You can add chopped fresh tomatoes, hardboiled eggs, and pita bread to scoop up all the flavorful goodness. This dish is sometimes spooned over Hummus (page 26) and called "hummus ful."

1 pound dried fava beans, rinsed and picked over

¼ cup olive oil

1 tablespoon tahini

2 teaspoons minced garlic

1 teaspoon ground cumin

½ teaspoon red pepper flakes

Juice of 1 lemon

Sea salt

1. Put the fava beans in a medium bowl and cover with about 2 inches of water. Set aside to soak overnight in the refrigerator.

2. Drain the beans, transfer them to a large saucepan, and cover them with about 2 inches of water.

3. Bring the beans to a boil and stir in the olive oil, tahini, garlic, cumin, and red pepper flakes. Reduce the heat to low and simmer until the beans are very tender and the mixture thickens, 50 to 55 minutes.

4. Remove from the heat and stir in the lemon juice and season with salt.

5. Serve.

COOKING TIP: Canned fava beans can be used in place of the dried beans to save time. Use two 15-ounce cans, drained, and add them to the sauce ingredients in step 3, then simmer for 20 minutes.

Lebanese Fried Eggs with Za'atar

SERVES 4 ♦ **PREP TIME:** 5 minutes ♦ **COOK TIME:** 6 minutes

Fried eggs become a culinary triumph when you add a generous sprinkling of za'atar seasoning. The citrus flavor and lovely spices are ideal with rich sunny-side-up yolks and whites with a tasty crisped edge. You can cook the eggs in butter instead of olive oil if you prefer.

2 tablespoons olive oil, divided	8 large eggs, divided	1 tablespoon Za'atar seasoning (page 146)

1. Heat 1 tablespoon of oil in a large skillet over medium heat and carefully crack in 4 eggs.

2. Let the eggs fry, tilting the pan occasionally to redistribute the uncooked whites until the edges are slightly crisp, and the yolk is cooked, about 2 minutes for runny yolks or 3 minutes for medium-firm yolks.

3. Transfer the eggs to two plates and set aside.

4. Repeat with the remaining 1 tablespoon of oil and the remaining 4 eggs and transfer to two additional plates.

5. Sprinkle the eggs with za'atar and serve.

MENU TIP: Serve this simple dish with a generous portion of Skillet Potatoes (Batata Harra) (page 52) or Mujadarra (page 44) to create a filling and attractive breakfast.

Turkish Börek

SERVES 4 ♦ **PREP TIME:** 30 minutes ♦ **COOK TIME:** 52 minutes

There is no breakfast dish in Western countries comparable to börek. The buttery pastry with melted cheeses and tender leeks is quite filling and rich, so pair it with some cut-up melon, orange slices, or berries to add a little freshness to the meal.

1 tablespoon olive oil, plus extra for greasing the baking dish

2 leeks, white and green parts, finely chopped

1 cup crumbled feta cheese

1 cup shredded mozzarella

1 tablespoon finely chopped fresh dill

¼ cup ghee

1 large egg

2 tablespoons plain yogurt

1 (16-ounce) package phyllo pastry

1 tablespoon black cumin seeds

1. Preheat the oven to 400°F and lightly grease a 9-by-13-inch glass baking dish with oil and set aside.

2. Heat the oil in a small skillet over medium-high heat and sauté the leeks until tender, 5 to 7 minutes.

3. Transfer the leeks to a medium bowl and stir in the feta, mozzarella, and dill until very well combined.

4. In a small bowl, whisk together the ghee, egg, and yogurt until blended.

5. Place a phyllo sheet on a clean work surface and brush it lightly with the butter mixture. Lay another sheet on the first and repeat with the butter mixture and phyllo until you have four stacked sheets. Repeat three times so that you have four sets of stacked sheets.

6. Transfer one set of stacked phyllo to the baking dish, arranging it so that any extra extends up the sides. Spread half of the cheese mixture on the phyllo.

7. Repeat with another stack of four phyllo sheets and the remaining cheese mixture. Top with the third stack of four phyllo sheets, tucking any over-hanging ends of phyllo into the sides of the baking dish.

8. Brush the top of the last phyllo stack with the butter mixture and scatter the cumin seeds all over.

9. Bake until the pastry is golden brown, 40 to 45 minutes.

10. Let the börek cool for 30 minutes and cut into squares to serve.

VARIATION TIP: Börek can be filled with minced meat, mushrooms, vegetables, mashed potatoes, or mashed chickpeas and prepared in rolled shapes, in neat square packets, or in a baking dish.

Golden Breakfast Porridge with Cinnamon and Sugar (Kachi)

SERVES 4 ♦ **PREP TIME:** 10 minutes ♦ **COOK TIME:** 23 minutes

While not porridge like traditional oatmeal, the texture of this dish is thick and filling when you need an excellent start to the morning. Classic Persian Kachi has a couple of teaspoons of rose water, as well as turmeric or saffron. This dish is served to boost energy and is often eaten when consuming something easy on the stomach is called for.

1½ cups water

1¼ cups sugar, divided

2 teaspoons turmeric or ¼ teaspoon ground saffron

½ cup butter

1 cup all-purpose flour

¼ teaspoon ground cinnamon, for garnish

1. Stir together the water and 1 cup of sugar in a small saucepan and bring to a boil over medium-high heat. Boil, stirring constantly, for 3 minutes.

2. Stir in the turmeric until the color is even and set aside off the heat.

3. Melt the butter in a large saucepan over medium heat and stir in the flour. Cook, stirring constantly, until the mixture is light brown, about 10 minutes.

4. Remove the flour mixture from the heat and whisk in the sugar syrup until completely incorporated.

5. Return the saucepan to medium heat and cook, whisking constantly until the mixture thickens, about 10 minutes.

6. Remove from the heat and spoon into four bowls.

7. Top with the remaining ¼ cup of sugar and sprinkle with cinnamon to serve.

FUN FACT: Turmeric is the secret ingredient in Kraft Dinner mac and cheese, used to create its signature bright color after the artificial dyes were removed. The flavor is mild enough that it doesn't affect the taste at all.

Moroccan Pancakes (Baghrir)

SERVES 4 ♦ **PREP TIME:** 15 minutes, plus rising time ♦ **COOK TIME:** 24 minutes

When you read this recipe, you might think the finished pancakes will look like crêpes, but these slightly sweet creations have a distinctive honeycomb pattern on the top. The tiny holes are ideal for catching all the luscious melted butter and honey used as a topping. The texture is unbelievably tender and lightly spongy. You might never make regular pancakes again!

2½ cups warm water
1 cup all-purpose flour
½ cup semolina

½ package (about
  1 teaspoon) dry yeast
1 teaspoon baking powder

4 tablespoons butter
4 tablespoons honey

1. In a large bowl, whisk together the water, flour, semolina, and yeast until smooth and well blended.

2. Whisk in the baking powder and leave the bowl in a warm place to let the batter thicken and rise, 30 to 40 minutes. The batter will be similar to crêpe batter.

3. Heat a medium (7-inch or 8-inch) nonstick skillet over medium heat until a water droplet sizzles when dripped into the skillet. Pour about ½ cup of batter into the skillet, tilting it so that the batter spreads thinly to the edges.

4. Cook until the pancake is cooked completely through, with tiny holes all over the surface, about 2 minutes.

5. Slide the pancake out onto a plate and cover with a clean cloth to keep warm.

6. Repeat with the remaining batter.

7. Serve topped with butter and honey.

MENU TIP: Chopped fresh fruit, whipped cream, date syrup, warm spices, condensed milk, and maple syrup (not traditional, but good) can all be used to top these delicious crêpe-like pancakes.

Moroccan Oatmeal (Hrbil)

SERVES 4 ♦ **PREP TIME:** 10 minutes ♦ **COOK TIME:** 55 minutes

Farro is used in place of the traditional wheat berries in this stick-to-your-ribs breakfast. Farro tastes slightly nutty and, similar to wheat berries, has a pleasantly chewy texture. Toasting the grains before slow cooking them in milk creates a sublime flavor, and the olive oil adds richness without an oily finish. You can also top the dish with maple syrup or a sprinkle of brown sugar.

1 cup farro or wheat berries

1 tablespoon olive oil

1 cup water

1 cup whole milk, plus more
   for serving

Sea salt

Butter, for serving

Honey, for serving

1. In a medium bowl, cover the farro with about 2 inches of water and soak overnight. Drain the grains when you are ready to cook them.

2. Heat the olive oil in a large saucepan over medium heat and sauté the soaked grains until lightly toasted, about 5 minutes.

3. Stir in the water and milk and bring the mixture to a boil. Reduce the heat to low and simmer, stirring occasionally, until most of the liquid is absorbed and the mixture is thick and creamy, about 50 minutes.

4. Season lightly with salt.

5. Serve with milk, butter, and a drizzle of honey.

COOKING TIP: If you want to cut the cooking time to about 20 minutes, purchase semi-pearled or pearled farro instead of whole grains.

Lamb Tagine,
page 116

Chapter Six

MAIN COURSES

Main courses are often served at lunchtime in the Middle East, as it is the biggest meal of the day. Dinner is typically lighter fare, eaten around 8:00 or 9:00 p.m., after evening prayers, and consisting of a salad or lunch leftovers. You can eat these dishes at whatever time suits your lifestyle, but leftovers are certainly an excellent option for a quick meal at a later time. Try combining these recipes with the rice, legume, and salad recipes in the other chapters, especially if you are entertaining guests.

Çiğ Köfte

SERVES 4 ♦ **PREP TIME:** 40 minutes, plus chilling time ♦ **COOK TIME:** 10 minutes

My mother was Dutch, so she had no issue eating raw hamburger or steak tartare while making dinner, which horrified my sister and me. Naturally, she was right at home eating the meat version of Turkish Çiğ köfte, with its spiced raw beef. This is a vegetarian recipe, with many of the same spices and flavors in a couscous and nut base.

1 cup water

1 cup dry couscous

½ cup chopped fresh mint

½ cup chopped
  fresh parsley

½ cup ground walnuts

¼ cup tomato paste

1 scallion, white and green
  parts, chopped

1 tablespoon olive oil

Juice and zest of ½ lemon

1 tablespoon paprika

2 teaspoons ground
  coriander

1 teaspoon ground cumin

¼ teaspoon red
  pepper flakes

Sea salt

4 pitas

1 cup shredded lettuce

1 large tomato, chopped

Lemon wedges

1. Bring a medium saucepan of water to a boil, then remove from heat. Stir in the couscous, cover, and set aside for 10 minutes.

2. Transfer the cooked couscous to a large bowl and fluff with a fork. Stir in the mint, parsley, walnuts, tomato paste, scallion, olive oil, lemon juice, lemon zest, paprika, coriander, cumin, and red pepper flakes until well combined.

3. Knead the mixture until it forms a paste that holds its shape when pressed. If it is too dry, add water by tablespoons to achieve the desired texture.

4. Let the mixture stand covered for 4 hours to firm up.

5. Use your hands to form the mixture into 4-inch-long cylinders, making sure to squeeze each cylinder between your palm and fingers to form finger marks. Repeat until the remaining mixture is used up.

6. Season the mixture with salt and serve wrapped in a pita bread topped with lettuce, tomato, and a squeeze of lemon juice.

MENU TIP: This dish has some heat, so it is often served with a cooling yogurt drink such as kefir or traditional ayran.

Sabich

SERVES 4 ♦ **PREP TIME:** 25 minutes ♦ **COOK TIME:** 5 minutes

Sabich is a street food that is enjoyed and valued for its crispy eggplant and tender hardboiled egg stuffing. When you add fresh tomatoes and tasty tahini sauce to the combination, the results are almost addictive. I often arrange bowls of the fillings, warmed pitas, and sauce for guests to enjoy during casual get-togethers, encouraging them to build their own sandwiches.

2 tablespoons olive oil

1 medium eggplant, cut into ½-inch rounds

Sea salt

1 English cucumber, diced

2 tomatoes, diced

Juice of 1 lemon

1 tablespoon chopped fresh parsley

4 pita bread, warmed

1 cup Hummus (page 26)

4 large hardboiled eggs, sliced

¼ cup Tahini Sauce (page 142)

1. Heat the oil in a large skillet over medium-high heat.

2. Season the eggplant slices lightly with salt.

3. Fry the eggplant slices until tender and golden brown, turning once, about 5 minutes total. Transfer the cooked eggplant to a paper-towel-lined plate and set aside.

4. While the eggplant is cooking, toss together the cucumber, tomatoes, lemon juice, and parsley in a small bowl.

5. Cut the pita bread in half, and open to form pockets.

6. Spread 2 tablespoons of hummus in each half and stuff the pockets with the eggplant, tomato salad, and sliced egg.

7. Drizzle with the tahini sauce and serve.

COOKING TIP: Fried eggs are sometimes used in place of the hardboiled eggs in this Israeli sandwich. Boiled potatoes are a common addition, as well.

Potato Pancakes (Kookoo Sib Zamini)

SERVES 4 ♦ **PREP TIME:** 15 minutes ♦ **COOK TIME:** 40 minutes

Potato pancakes show up in many cultures because they are inexpensive and filling. These are denser pancakes, unlike lacy latkes, so they could undoubtedly be a fantastic main meal. Serve them with a topping of tart yogurt, sliced tomatoes, and diced cucumber.

1 pound russet potatoes, peeled and cut into 2-inch chunks

3 large eggs, beaten

1 tablespoon all-purpose flour

1 teaspoon baking powder

½ teaspoon ground cumin

½ teaspoon ground turmeric

Sea salt

Freshly ground black pepper

¼ cup sunflower or vegetable oil

1. Put the potatoes in a large saucepan and cover with about 2 inches of water.

2. Bring to a boil over high heat, reduce the heat to low, and simmer until the potatoes are tender but not mushy, about 30 minutes.

3. Drain the potatoes and set aside to cool in a large bowl.

4. Mash the potatoes or grate them with a box grater. Stir in the eggs, flour, baking powder, cumin, and turmeric until well mixed. Season with salt and pepper.

5. Divide the potato mixture into 8 pieces and form them into patties, about ½ inch thick.

6. Heat the oil in a large skillet over medium heat and fry the patties until golden on both sides, turning once, about 10 minutes in total.

7. Serve warm.

COOKING TIP: You can cook the potatoes ahead of time and store them in a container in the refrigerator for up to 3 days.

Koshari

SERVES 4 ♦ **PREP TIME:** 25 minutes ♦ **COOK TIME:** 55 minutes

Koshari, also spelled kushari or koshary, is the national dish of Egypt for very good reason. The recipe has several individual elements such as the legumes, grains, pasta, and fried onions, as well as a tart tomato sauce. Try it and see why koshari can be found everywhere in Egypt, from restaurants to home kitchens.

4 cups water

1 cup dried lentils, picked through and rinsed

1 cup basmati rice

1 cup dry pasta shells

1 tablespoon olive oil

1 small sweet onion

1 tablespoon minced garlic

1 (28-ounce) can low-sodium diced tomatoes

1 teaspoon white or apple cider vinegar

1 teaspoon ground cumin

¼ teaspoon red pepper flakes

Sea salt

Freshly ground black pepper

2 cups Crispy Fried Onions (page 145)

1. Bring the water and lentils to a boil in a large saucepan. Reduce the heat to low, cover, and simmer until the lentils are tender, about 30 minutes.

2. Stir in the rice, cover, and continue simmering until the rice is cooked, about 25 minutes more.

3. While the lentils and rice are cooking, bring a second medium saucepan filled with water to a boil over high heat and cook the pasta according to package directions, about 20 minutes.

4. While the pasta is cooking, heat the oil in a medium skillet over medium-high heat. Sauté the onion and garlic until softened, about 3 minutes.

5. Strain the pasta and transfer to a large bowl. When the lentils and rice are cooked, drain any excess water and add to the bowl with the pasta, stirring to mix.

6. Stir the tomatoes, vinegar, cumin, and red pepper flakes in with the onion and garlic mixture, and bring to a boil. Reduce the heat to low and simmer the sauce until the flavors mellow and it thickens slightly, about 15 minutes.

CONTINUED ▶

7. Scoop a generous portion of the lentil mixture onto plates, season with salt and pepper, and top with the tomato sauce and fried onions.

8. Serve.

FUN FACT: This dish has its origins in an Indian dish composed of rice and lentils, brought to Egypt by Indian soldiers serving the British during World War I. It evolved with the addition of the regional spices and pasta over the subsequent decades.

Crunchy Baked Saffron Rice with Barberries (Tachin)

SERVES 4 ♦ **PREP TIME:** 20 minutes ♦ **COOK TIME:** 1 hour and 33 minutes

Tachin is a Persian creation that is basically a creamy rice cake with crispy edges that can include other elements such as chicken, meats, fish, and vegetables. This sweeter version with tart barberries and saffron is quite traditional. Keep an eye on your finished tachin—my sons always pick off the delicious crispy sides before I can get it on the table.

¼ cup boiling water

Pinch saffron threads

1 tablespoon olive oil, plus extra for greasing the baking dish

½ sweet onion, chopped

1 cup basmati rice, rinsed

2 cups chicken broth

¾ cup plain yogurt

2 egg yolks

½ cup dried barberries or cherries

¼ cup pine nuts

Sea salt

Freshly ground black pepper

1. Preheat the oven to 400°F.

2. Lightly grease a 9-by-9-inch baking dish and set aside.

3. In a small bowl, stir together the boiling water and saffron and let stand 5 minutes to steep.

4. Heat the oil in a large saucepan over medium-high heat and sauté the onion until softened, about 3 minutes.

5. Stir in the rice, saffron mixture, and chicken broth and bring the mixture to a boil. Reduce the heat, cover, and simmer until the rice is cooked and the liquid absorbed, about 25 minutes.

6. While the rice is cooking, in a medium bowl, stir together the yogurt, egg yolks, dried barberries, and pine nuts.

7. Stir the cooked rice into the yogurt mixture until well combined. Season with salt and pepper.

8. Spoon the rice mixture into the baking dish, spreading it out evenly and pressing it down firmly.

CONTINUED ▶

9. Cover the baking dish with a lid or aluminum foil and bake until the rice is golden and crispy around all the edges, about 1 hour.

10. Cool the rice, then run a knife around the edges to loosen the rice and invert onto a plate to serve.

COOKING TIP: Dried barberries can be found in some international markets or online at retailers such as Amazon. For a less chewy texture, you can soak the dried berries in hot water for 10 minutes to reconstitute them before using them in this dish.

Masgouf

SERVES 4 ♦ **PREP TIME:** 15 minutes, plus marinating time ♦ **COOK TIME:** 8 minutes

Masgouf, a national dish of Iraq, is all about the tenderness of freshly caught fish. So, whenever possible, pick fish from a tank in a fish market and cook them on the same day. Traditional Masgouf recipes are for grilled fish rather than broiled, so try that method if you have a grill.

Juice of 1 lemon, divided

3 teaspoons curry powder, divided

2 teaspoons olive oil, divided

4 (5-ounce) skinless halibut fillets

2 tomatoes, diced

½ red onion, thinly sliced

Sea salt

1. In a medium bowl, stir together half the lemon juice, 1½ teaspoons curry powder, and 1 teaspoon olive oil.

2. Pat the fish dry with paper towels and add the fillets to the bowl, turning to coat.

3. Cover and refrigerate for 30 minutes.

4. In a small bowl, mix together the tomatoes, onion, remaining half of the lemon juice, remaining 1½ teaspoons of curry powder, and remaining 1 teaspoon of oil. Season the mixture with salt and set aside.

5. Preheat the oven to broil.

6. Place the fish on a small baking sheet and evenly divide the tomato mixture among the fish, spreading it out on top of each fillet.

7. Broil until the fish flakes easily with a fork, 6 to 8 minutes.

8. Serve.

VARIATION TIP: The traditional fish used in this dish is often carp, which can be difficult to find in most fish markets in North America. Additions to the recipe can include turmeric, paprika, red pepper flakes, or tamarind for an appealing sweetness.

Fish Harrah

SERVES 4 ♦ **PREP TIME:** 20 minutes ♦ **COOK TIME:** 40 minutes

Fish Harrah means "spicy fish" in Arabic. I remember when I was a teenager being taken aback by the whole fish with the head attached and its cloudy eyes. You do not have to use a whole fish, even though it is traditional. It can be disconcerting when your meal is looking back at you.

4 pounds whole fish, cleaned

3 tablespoons olive oil, divided, plus extra for greasing the baking sheet

Sea salt

1 red bell pepper, chopped

1 large red chile pepper, seeded and chopped

1 tablespoon minced garlic

2 teaspoons ground coriander

1 cup low-sodium chicken broth

½ cup chopped fresh cilantro

Juice of 2 lemons

2 tablespoons chopped fresh parsley, for garnish

1. Preheat the oven to 350°F.

2. Lightly oil a baking sheet with a lip, or a large baking dish with olive oil.

3. Pat the fish dry with a paper towel and place them on the baking sheet. Brush the fish with 1 tablespoon of olive oil and lightly season with salt.

4. Bake the fish until it is just cooked through, about 30 minutes.

5. While the fish is baking, heat the remaining 2 tablespoons of oil in a medium skillet over medium-high heat.

6. Sauté the bell pepper, chile pepper, garlic, and coriander until the vegetables are tender, about 3 minutes.

7. Stir in the broth, cilantro, and lemon juice and bring the mixture to a boil. Remove from the heat and set aside until the fish is cooked.

8. Pour the sauce over the fish and return to the oven for 10 minutes.

9. Serve topped with parsley.

COOKING TIP: Try using haddock, halibut, bass, or snapper. Many grocery stores stock whole trout, sometimes in tanks, so this can also be a great choice if you ask the fish monger to clean the trout and leave it whole.

Middle Eastern Fish Pilaf (Sayyadieh)

SERVES 4 ♦ **PREP TIME:** 20 minutes ♦ **COOK TIME:** 42 minutes

The countries that line the coasts of the Mediterranean Sea, the Arabian Sea, and the Red Sea have the luxury of enjoying unbelievable seafood, often daily. The success of this pilaf depends on good-quality fish and perfectly caramelized onions. You can prepare the fish in the rice, but it is especially delicious when lightly battered and fried to a perfect golden brown.

For the rice

2 tablespoons oil

1 sweet onion, chopped

1 teaspoon peeled and grated fresh ginger

1 teaspoon ground cumin

½ teaspoon ground cinnamon

⅛ teaspoon ground cloves

2 cups low-sodium chicken broth

1 cup white rice, rinsed

For the fish

1 pound catfish fillets, cut into 4-inch pieces

Sea salt

Freshly ground black pepper

1 cup all-purpose flour

¼ cup vegetable oil

To make the rice

1. Heat the oil in a medium saucepan over medium-high heat.

2. Sauté the onion until caramelized, about 10 minutes.

3. Stir in the ginger, cumin, cinnamon, and cloves, and sauté 2 minutes more.

4. Stir in the broth and rice and bring to a boil.

5. Reduce the heat to low, cover, and simmer until the rice is tender and the liquid is absorbed, 25 to 30 minutes.

6. Remove from the heat and set aside.

CONTINUED ▶

To make the fish

1. Pat the fish dry with paper towels and lightly season with salt and pepper.

2. Spread the flour on a small plate and dredge the fish pieces in the flour, shaking off any excess.

3. Heat the oil in a large skillet over medium-high heat.

4. Fry the fish pieces until golden brown and cooked through, turning once, 6 to 7 minutes in total.

5. Serve the fish on a bed of rice.

COOKING TIP: Use the freshest fish possible to create the recipe as it is intended, a dish that highlights the texture and flavor of fish.

Fried Fish (Samak Maqli)

SERVES 4 ♦ **PREP TIME:** 20 minutes plus marinating time ♦ **COOK TIME:** 8 minutes

Trout is an ideal fish for this Lebanese dish because it is firm; its sweet flesh holds up beautifully when lightly battered and fried. I tried this dish using trout caught right out of a sparkling North American lake and prepared as a shore lunch over a campfire. I don't think I have ever tasted anything so amazing, with such a perfect balance of spices.

Juice from 1 lemon
½ teaspoon garlic powder
¼ teaspoon ground ginger
¼ teaspoon ground coriander

¼ teaspoon ground cumin
⅛ teaspoon sea salt
⅛ teaspoon freshly ground black pepper

1 pound boneless skinless trout
1 cup all-purpose flour
¼ cup vegetable oil
Lemon wedges, for serving

1. In a medium bowl, stir together the lemon juice, garlic powder, ginger, coriander, cumin, salt, and pepper.

2. Pat the fish dry with paper towels and add the fillets to the bowl, turning to coat. Let the fish marinate for 30 minutes.

3. Pour the flour on a plate. Dredge the marinated fish pieces in the flour and set aside.

4. Heat the oil in a large skillet over medium-high heat and fry the fish until golden brown and cooked through, turning once, 7 to 8 minutes in total.

5. Serve with lemon wedges.

MENU TIP: Serve this fish with Tabbouleh (page 45), Lebanese Rice (page 53), or Harissa-Roasted Cauliflower (page 57) for a lovely full meal. You can also fold this crispy fish into a pita with some chopped vegetables for a grab-and-go option.

Fish Cakes

SERVES 4 ♦ **PREP TIME:** 15 minutes ♦ **COOK TIME:** 10 minutes

Don't let the unassuming title of this recipe fool you; these are not fish cakes you might have had in the past. Tender white fish, fresh herbs, and a generous amount of spices ensure this dish is exceptional. This Israeli-inspired dish can be served with a yogurt garlic sauce (see page 120) or drizzled with Tahini Sauce (page 142).

1½ pounds boneless skinless halibut or grouper, cut into large chunks
1 large egg
½ sweet onion, chopped
1 tablespoon minced garlic

¾ cup bread crumbs or almond meal
¼ cup chopped fresh cilantro
2 teaspoons Ras El Hanout (page 151)

¼ teaspoon sea salt
¼ teaspoon freshly ground black pepper
Olive oil, for frying

1. Put the fish, egg, onion, garlic, bread crumbs, cilantro, Ras El Hanout, salt, and pepper in a food processor and pulse until the mixture forms a thick paste.

2. Divide the mixture into 8 equal pieces and form them into fish cakes about ¾ inch thick.

3. Heat about 1 inch of oil in a medium skillet over medium-high heat and deep fry the fish cakes, turning once, until they are golden brown and cooked through, 8 to 10 minutes in total.

4. Serve.

COOKING TIP: This recipe can be made ahead. Freeze the raw patties on a baking sheet and then transfer to freezer bags. Store in the freezer for up to 3 months, thaw when you want to use them, and fry as specified in the recipe.

Middle Eastern Lamb Kebabs

SERVES 4 ♦ **PREP TIME:** 20 minutes, plus marinating time ♦ **COOK TIME:** 8 minutes

Even if you know nothing about Middle Eastern cuisine, you are likely familiar with kebabs. This kebab is not one from a specific region or country, so there is lots of room to play with the ingredients. If you enjoy this dish and want to make it regularly, invest in metal skewers. Wooden skewers need to be soaked ahead of time and can still burn on a grill.

1 sweet onion, cut into eighths

2 garlic cloves, crushed

Juice and zest of 1 lemon

1 tablespoon chopped parsley

½ teaspoon ground cumin

½ teaspoon ground allspice

½ teaspoon sea salt

1 pound lamb loin, trimmed of fat and cut into 1-inch cubes

2 tablespoons olive oil

4 pita bread, warmed and halved

½ cup plain Greek yogurt

1. Put the onion, garlic, lemon juice, lemon zest, parsley, cumin, allspice, and salt in a blender and pulse until the mixture is smooth.

2. Pour the marinade into a medium bowl, add the lamb chunks, and turn to coat the meat.

3. Cover the bowl with plastic wrap and marinate the lamb in the refrigerator for at least 6 hours.

4. Preheat a grill to medium-high heat.

5. Thread the lamb onto 8 skewers, shaking off any extra marinade, and brush the skewers with the olive oil.

6. Grill the lamb (or broil in an oven), turning several times until the meat is lightly charred and medium, about 8 minutes in total.

7. Serve stuffed into pitas with a scoop of yogurt.

VARIATION TIP: Generally, you can use chicken, beef, and vegetables such as eggplant, zucchini, tomatoes, onions, and potatoes. The rubs and marinades should be spicy and contain some of the choices listed in the first chapter of this book (see page 9).

Herb Meatballs
in Tomato-Plum Sauce (Kufte)

SERVES 4 ♦ **PREP TIME:** 25 minutes ♦ **COOK TIME:** 60 minutes

Kufte is a Persian meatball with some unusual ingredients such as lentils, rice, and a dried plum in the middle. The combination of savory meat and sweet fruit is inspired, especially when added to the delectable tomato sauce.

1 pound lean ground beef

1 cup cooked lentils

½ cup cooked
long-grain rice

1 large egg

1 scallion, white and green
parts, chopped

¼ cup chopped
fresh parsley

¼ cup chopped fresh dill

2 teaspoons turmeric

Sea salt

Freshly ground
black pepper

12 small pitted prunes

¼ cup olive oil, divided

1 sweet onion, chopped

3 cups low-sodium
chicken broth

1 cup diced tomatoes

⅓ cup tomato paste

1. In a large bowl, combine the beef, lentils, rice, egg, scallion, parsley, dill, and turmeric until very well mixed. Season with salt and pepper.

2. Divide the meat mixture into 8 equal pieces and roll into balls. Push a prune into the center of each meatball. Set aside and chop the remaining prunes.

3. Heat 2 tablespoons of oil in a large saucepan over medium-high heat. Sauté the onions until softened, about 3 minutes.

4. Stir in the broth, chopped prunes, tomatoes, and tomato paste and bring the mixture to a boil. Reduce the heat to medium-low and simmer the sauce until it thickens slightly, about 5 minutes.

5. Heat the remaining 2 tablespoons of oil in a large skillet over medium-high heat and brown the meatballs on all sides, about 10 minutes in total.

6. Add the browned meatballs to the sauce and simmer until they are cooked through and tender, about 40 minutes. Serve.

FUN FACT: The technique and practice of drying plums is thought to have originated in the Caspian Sea area thousands of years ago.

Kibbeh

SERVES 4 ♦ **PREP TIME:** 25 minutes ♦ **COOK TIME:** 55 minutes

Kibbeh is found in many Middle Eastern countries such as Syria, Lebanon, Iraq, Iran, and Egypt. This is an easy casserole version of a spicy bulgur and meat recipe, so you can experience the textures and flavors without having to form the mixtures into croquettes and fry them.

For the filling

1 tablespoon olive oil

1 sweet onion, chopped

½ pound ground beef

½ teaspoon ground cinnamon

½ teaspoon ground allspice

¼ teaspoon sea salt

¼ teaspoon freshly ground black pepper

¼ cup pine nuts

For the bulgur mixture

Oil, for greasing the baking dish

1 cup fine bulgur

1 pound ground beef

1 sweet onion, finely chopped

½ teaspoon ground cinnamon

½ teaspoon ground allspice

¼ teaspoon sea salt

½ teaspoon freshly ground black pepper

To make the filling

1. Heat the oil in a large skillet over medium-high heat and sauté the onion until softened, about 3 minutes.

2. Stir in the beef, cinnamon, allspice, salt, and pepper and cook until the beef is completely cooked through, about 7 minutes.

3. Stir in the pine nuts and set aside.

To make the bulgur mixture

1. Preheat the oven to 400°F. Lightly grease a 9-by-13-inch baking dish with oil and set aside.

2. Pour the bulgur into a large bowl and cover with about 2 inches of boiling water. Let stand for 10 minutes. Drain the excess water from the bowl.

CONTINUED ▶

3. Put the beef, onion, cinnamon, allspice, salt, and pepper in a food processor and pulse to make a smooth, well-combined paste.

4. Transfer the meat mixture to the bulgur and mix with your hands to combine.

5. Press half the bulgur mixture into the baking dish to form a layer on the bottom and up the sides.

6. Spoon the filling onto the bulgur layer, spreading it out evenly.

7. Top with an even layer of the remaining bulgur mixture.

8. Score the top in a diagonal crosshatch pattern with a small knife.

9. Bake until cooked through and browned, 40 to 45 minutes.

10. Serve.

FUN FACT: Camel is a traditional choice for the meat in kibbeh. Camel tastes very much like lean beef, although it can taste a bit gamey when the camel is older.

Lamb Köfte

SERVES 4 ♦ **PREP TIME:** 25 minutes, plus chilling time ♦ **COOK TIME:** 15 minutes

Technically, these tender kebabs are just meatballs in another form, simple to make and delicious to eat. My favorite way to eat the kebabs is sizzling right off a grill with fresh flatbread, yogurt, and a spoonful of chopped tomato.

1 pound ground lamb

½ sweet onion, grated

1 large egg

2 teaspoons minced garlic

2 tablespoons finely chopped parsley

1 tablespoon finely chopped mint

½ teaspoon ground cumin

½ teaspoon ground coriander

½ teaspoon ground cinnamon

Sea salt

1. In a large bowl, combine the lamb, onion, egg, garlic, parsley, mint, cumin, coriander, and cinnamon.

2. Mix together very well using your hands and season with salt.

3. Divide the lamb mixture into 4 equal pieces and shape them into long cylinders.

4. Push the cylinders onto 4 metal skewers, spreading them along most of the length.

5. Chill the meat skewers in the refrigerator for 1 hour.

6. Preheat a grill to medium heat and grill the skewers, turning several times, until the meat is lightly charred and cooked through, 12 to 15 minutes in total.

7. Season with salt and serve.

COOKING TIP: If you do not have a grill, you can broil these skewers in the oven for about 10 to 12 minutes total, turning once.

Spiced Beef Tagine

SERVES 4 ♦ **PREP TIME:** 15 minutes ♦ **COOK TIME:** 35 minutes

I prepared this dish for my boss in Tripoli, sweating in 127°F weather, which was the outside temperature, not the ambient temperature in my hot kitchen. The cooking method in a sealed container over low heat meant the preparation did not spike the temperature higher, and as a bonus, this enclosed method creates meltingly tender meat.

2 tablespoons olive oil, divided

1 pound ground beef

1 eggplant, peeled and cut into 1-inch chunks

2 zucchini, cut into ½-inch rounds

1 tablespoon minced garlic

1 tablespoon peeled and grated fresh ginger

1 tablespoon Ras El Hanout (page 151)

1 tablespoon Harissa (page 148)

1 (15-ounce) can low-sodium diced tomatoes

1 cup low-sodium canned chickpeas, rinsed and drained

1 tablespoon chopped fresh parsley, for seasoning

1. Heat 1 tablespoon olive oil in a large saucepan over medium-high heat. Sauté the beef until it is cooked through, about 8 minutes. Transfer the beef to a plate using a slotted spoon and set aside.

2. Add the remaining 1 tablespoon of olive oil and sauté the eggplant for 10 minutes. Stir in the zucchini, garlic, ginger, Ras El Hanout, and harissa, and sauté for 2 minutes. Stir in the reserved beef, tomatoes, and chickpeas.

3. Bring the mixture to a boil, then reduce the heat to low and simmer, covered, until the eggplant is tender, about 15 minutes.

4. Serve topped with parsley.

COOKING TIP: Instead of simmering the dish, you can cover an oven-proof skillet and bake in a 400°F oven for 20 to 25 minutes.

Maqlooba (Maqluba)

SERVES 4 ♦ **PREP TIME:** 25 minutes ♦ **COOK TIME:** 58 minutes

The presentation of Maqlooba might be the most fun in this entire book, and the one most fraught with the prospect of something going wrong. You will be flipping the finished dish over to create a layered tower that depends entirely on how firmly you make the layers. Don't worry if yours collapses; everything will still be delicious.

2 tablespoons olive oil, plus extra for greasing the saucepan
1 sweet onion, chopped
1 teaspoon minced garlic
1 pound ground beef
1 teaspoon ground allspice
¼ teaspoon ground cinnamon

3 tomatoes, thinly sliced
4 cups diced mixed vegetables (red bell pepper, zucchini, cauliflower, eggplant)
2 cups basmati rice
3 cups hot low-sodium chicken stock
¼ cup pine nuts

2 tablespoons chopped fresh parsley
Sea salt
Freshly ground black pepper

1. Heat the olive oil in the large skillet over medium-high heat.

2. Sauté the onion and garlic until softened, about 3 minutes.

3. Stir in the beef, allspice, and cinnamon and sauté until the meat is browned and cooked through and any liquid is evaporated, about 12 minutes.

4. Lightly grease a large saucepan with olive oil and arrange the tomato slices in a layer on the bottom of the saucepan. Add the meat mixture and press down to flatten. Top with the mixed vegetables and press down to pack all the ingredients tightly.

5. Top with the rice, pressing down to flatten.

6. Slowly pour the stock over the ingredients, using the back of a spoon to avoid washing the rice away. Place the saucepan on high heat until you can see the broth simmering around the edges, about 3 minutes.

7. Cover, and reduce the heat to low, and cook until the rice is tender, about 40 minutes.

CONTINUED ▶

8. Place a serving plate over the top of the saucepan and invert the contents onto the plate. It should stay intact.

9. Garnish with pine nuts and parsley, and season with salt and pepper.

10. Serve.

FUN FACT: The name *maqluba* means "upside-down" in Arabic, which is appropriate considering you literally flip this dish over to serve it like an upside-down cake.

Spiced Beef Sausage (Merguez)

SERVES 4 ♦ **PREP TIME:** 15 minutes, plus chilling time ♦ **COOK TIME:** 20 minutes

I did not cook with beef very much in North Africa, as it was not an easily obtained ingredient. When I did find ground beef, I often made heavily spiced sausages to grill or fry for my restaurant clientele. You won't have to deal with casings in this recipe because the meat mixture is formed into plump patties instead.

1 pound ground beef

¾ cup bread crumbs

3 tablespoons Harissa (page 148)

1 tablespoon minced garlic

2 teaspoons fennel seeds

2 teaspoons ground cumin

1 teaspoon ground coriander

1 teaspoon ground cinnamon

½ teaspoon smoked paprika

½ teaspoon sea salt

2 tablespoons olive oil

1. In a large bowl, mix together the beef, bread crumbs, harissa, garlic, fennel, cumin, coriander, cinnamon, paprika, and salt until very well combined.

2. Divide the mixture into 8 equal pieces and roll them into balls. Press the balls down to form patties ½ inch thick and set them on a plate. Cover the patties with plastic wrap and refrigerate for 1 hour to mellow the flavors.

3. Preheat the oven to 400°F and line a baking sheet with parchment paper.

4. Heat the oil in a large skillet over medium-high heat and brown the patties on both sides, flipping once, about 10 minutes in total.

5. Transfer the patties to the baking sheet and bake until cooked through, about 10 minutes.

6. Serve.

COOKING TIP: Form the meat mixture into long kebabs on metal skewers and grill them instead of baking them in the oven. Then serve them stuffed into pita bread with freshly chopped tomato.

Ground Beef with Pine Nuts (Lebanese Hashweh)

SERVES 4 ♦ **PREP TIME:** 5 minutes ♦ **COOK TIME:** 15 minutes

If new to Middle Eastern cooking, this is the ideal recipe to start with because it uses a few common ingredients and a skillet. The dish tastes more complicated than you might imagine, with balanced spices, crunchy pine nuts, and fresh, earthy parsley. You can serve the meat over a fluffy bowl of rice or couscous for a more substantial meal.

1 tablespoon olive oil

1 pound ground beef

1 sweet onion, chopped

1 tablespoon Bahārāt (page 147)

½ cup toasted pine nuts

2 tablespoons chopped fresh parsley

1. Heat the oil in a large skillet over medium-high heat and cook the beef, onion, and Bahārāt until the beef is cooked through and browned, 12 to 15 minutes.

2. Stir in the pine nuts and parsley.

3. Serve.

MENU TIP: This flavorful meat mixture can be tucked into a pita or folded in a flatbread to create a simple lunch or snack. Add a scoop of yogurt and shredded lettuce for a real treat.

Arabic Meat in Yogurt Sauce (Shakriya)

SERVES 4 ♦ **PREP TIME:** 10 minutes ♦ **COOK TIME:** 1 hour and 18 minutes

There is no comparable recipe in Western cooking to this creation. You can use lamb for the recipe because the stronger flavor of that meat will not overpower the tasty yogurt sauce. Serve this dish over fluffy basmati rice, nutty bulgur, or golden couscous.

2 tablespoons olive oil

1 pound beef sirloin, trimmed of fat and cubed

1 tablespoon minced garlic

4 cups low-sodium beef broth

1 bay leaf

3 tablespoons water

3 tablespoons cornstarch

3 cups plain yogurt

Sea salt

1. Heat the oil in a large saucepan over medium-high heat.

2. Sauté the beef until completely browned, about 10 minutes.

3. Add the garlic and sauté 3 minutes more.

4. Stir in the broth and bay leaf and bring to a boil. Reduce the heat to low and simmer until the meat is very tender, about 1 hour. Remove the bay leaf.

5. In a small bowl, stir together the water and cornstarch to create a slurry.

6. Stir the yogurt and slurry into the meat. Simmer over low heat until the soup thickens slightly, about 5 minutes.

7. Season with salt and serve.

VARIATION TIP: The slurry can be made with flour, arrowroot, or potato starch instead of cornstarch to thicken this dish.

Lamb Tagine

SERVES 4 ♦ **PREP TIME:** 15 minutes, plus marinating time
♦ **COOK TIME:** 2 hours and 20 minutes

While this recipe looks intimidating because the ingredient list is long, it is really just lamb, vegetables, broth, and heaps of spices for the marinade. After making the marinade, there is barely anything left to mix up! Marinating the lamb (or you can try beef) is the secret to infusing the meat with as much flavor as possible, as well as browning it to seal in all that spicy goodness.

3 tablespoons olive oil, divided

1 teaspoon paprika

1 teaspoon ground cinnamon

½ teaspoon ground coriander

½ teaspoon ground ginger

½ teaspoon ground cardamom

¼ teaspoon ground cumin

¼ teaspoon sea salt

¼ teaspoon ground turmeric

¼ teaspoon cayenne pepper

⅛ teaspoon ground cloves

1 pound lamb shoulder, cut into 1-inch cubes

2 carrots, thinly sliced

1 sweet onion, diced

2 teaspoons minced garlic

2 teaspoons peeled and grated fresh ginger

2 cups low-sodium chicken broth

2 tablespoons tomato paste

Zest of 1 lemon

1 tablespoon honey

1. Stir together 2 tablespoons olive oil, paprika, cinnamon, coriander, ginger, cardamom, cumin, salt, turmeric, cayenne pepper, and cloves in a large bowl and add the lamb. Toss to coat, cover, and refrigerate for at least 8 hours.

2. Heat the remaining 1 tablespoon of olive oil in a large skillet over medium-high heat. Sauté the lamb in batches until browned on all sides, about 15 minutes. Remove the lamb to a plate using a slotted spoon.

3. Stir in the carrots, onion, garlic, and ginger and sauté for 5 minutes.

4. Return the lamb to the skillet and stir in the broth, tomato paste, zest, and honey. Bring to a boil, reduce heat to low, cover, and simmer until the lamb is very tender, stirring occasionally, 1½ to 2 hours.

5. Serve.

VARIATION TIP: Try pomegranate molasses, date paste, or dried apricots instead of honey to create a lovely sweet note in this dish.

Chicken Kabsa

SERVES 4 ♦ **PREP TIME:** 15 minutes ♦ **COOK TIME:** 1 hour and 5 minutes

Basmati *means "sweet smell," which is apropos because this rice is very fragrant when cooked. The rice in this recipe is cooked in the cooking liquid, so it is exceptionally flavorful. You might start eating it before completing the dish!*

¼ cup olive oil, divided

1 pound boneless chicken thighs and breasts, cut into 3-inch pieces

1 sweet onion, thinly sliced

1 cup grated carrot

2 teaspoons chopped garlic

1 cup low-sodium crushed tomatoes

1 cup chopped tomatoes

1 cup low-sodium chicken broth

Zest of 1 orange

4 whole cloves

2 cinnamon sticks

1 cup basmati rice

¼ cup golden raisins

¼ cup chopped pistachios

1. Heat 2 tablespoons of oil over medium-high heat and sauté the chicken until it is golden and cooked halfway through, about 10 minutes.

2. Remove the chicken to a plate using a slotted spoon and set aside.

3. Add the remaining 2 tablespoons of oil and sauté the onion, carrot, and garlic until tender, about 4 minutes.

4. Stir in the crushed tomatoes, chopped tomatoes, broth, zest, cloves, cinnamon, and reserved chicken.

5. Bring to a boil, reduce the heat to medium, cover, and cook until the chicken is completely cooked through, about 25 minutes.

6. Remove the chicken back to the plate using a slotted spoon, cover with foil to keep warm, and remove the cinnamon sticks and cloves.

7. Stir the rice into the liquid in the skillet, cover, and simmer until the rice is tender and the liquid is absorbed, 25 to 30 minutes.

8. Spoon the rice onto a serving plate and top with the chicken.

9. Top with raisins and pistachios and serve.

MENU TIP: Serve this delightful creation with the fresh tomato and cucumber Shirazi Salad (page 51) and add a spoonful of Red Chile Pepper Paste (Shatta) (page 150) for a real taste explosion.

Iraqi Yellow Spice-Rubbed Chicken (Djaj Bil-Bahar Il-Asfar)

SERVES 4 ♦ **PREP TIME:** 10 minutes, plus chilling time ♦ **COOK TIME:** 42 minutes

It is impossible to describe the mouthwatering scent of this chicken. The spice mix might seem like a lot, but the poultry should be coated in it, not just sprinkled. If the spices are falling off, add a couple tablespoons of olive oil to form a paste. Serve with Tabbouleh (page 45) or Fattoush (page 47).

4 dried chile peppers

1 teaspoon coriander seeds

1 teaspoon cumin seeds

1 teaspoon whole
   black peppercorns

4 cloves

2 tablespoons minced garlic

2 teaspoons
   ground cinnamon

2 teaspoons ground nutmeg

1 teaspoon ground ginger

1 teaspoon ground
   cardamom

1 teaspoon ground allspice

1 teaspoon curry powder

1 teaspoon ground
   fenugreek

2 pounds boneless skinless
   chicken thighs

Flatbread, such as naan,
   for serving

1. Combine the chiles, coriander, cumin, peppercorns, and cloves in a medium skillet over medium heat and cook, swirling the skillet, until the seeds pop, about 2 minutes.

2. Cool the spices, then transfer them to a coffee or spice grinder and grind.

3. Transfer the spices to a medium bowl and stir in the garlic, cinnamon, nutmeg, ginger, cardamom, allspice, curry powder, and fenugreek. Add the chicken and toss to coat.

4. Cover the bowl and refrigerate overnight.

5. Preheat a grill to medium-high.

6. Grill the chicken until it is lightly charred and cooked through, turning once, 35 to 40 minutes, or until the internal temperature is 165°F. (If you do not have a grill, preheat an oven to 375°F and cook for 40 to 45 minutes.)

7. Serve the chicken with the flatbread.

FUN FACT: Fenugreek was originally used in embalming fluid by the Egyptians. Its sweet scent masked other more unpleasant smells during the ceremony.

Chicken Shawarma

SERVES 4 ♦ **PREP TIME:** 15 minutes, plus chilling time ♦ **COOK TIME:** 30 minutes

You may be familiar with this dish, as chicken shawarma has become mainstream in North America. I make shawarma when I need something in a hurry that will fill my family up—and they won't complain about it, because it tastes so good!

½ cup olive oil, plus extra for greasing a baking sheet

Juice of 1 lemon

2 tablespoons Shawarma Spice (page 149)

1 tablespoon minced garlic

1 pound boneless skinless chicken thighs

1 onion, thinly sliced

4 pitas, warmed and halved

2 cups shredded lettuce

1 cup chopped tomatoes

1 cup chopped cucumbers

Yogurt garlic sauce (see page 120)

1. In a large bowl, stir together the oil, lemon juice, shawarma spice, and garlic.

2. Add the chicken and toss to coat. Cover and refrigerate for at least 4 hours.

3. Preheat the oven to 400°F.

4. Grease a baking sheet with olive oil.

5. Transfer the chicken and marinade to the baking sheet, add the onion, and toss to coat.

6. Bake until the chicken is cooked through and golden, about 30 minutes.

7. Let the chicken stand for 10 minutes, then slice it thinly.

8. Evenly divide the chicken and onion mixture among the pitas. Stuff the pitas with the lettuce, tomatoes, and cucumbers, and top with yogurt sauce.

9. Serve.

VARIATION TIP: Israeli shawarma is made from turkey instead of chicken and, due to dietary restrictions, is served with a rich tahini sauce instead of yogurt (dairy).

Lebanese Chicken Fatteh

SERVES 4 ♦ **PREP TIME:** 15 minutes ♦ **COOK TIME:** 20 minutes

"Bowls" are a trendy culinary presentation of many ingredients arranged in layers in one bowl. This dish was a "bowl" before such things were fashionable, containing a combination of ingredients such as legumes, chicken, and nuts, all piled together in a delicious hodgepodge.

For the fatteh

1 (15-ounce) can low-sodium chickpeas, rinsed and drained

2 pita breads, cut into 1-inch pieces and toasted

½ cup toasted pine nuts

½ cup slivered almonds

1 tablespoon olive oil

1 pound boneless skinless chicken breast, cut into 1-inch strips

½ teaspoon garlic powder

½ teaspoon ground cardamom

½ teaspoon ground coriander

½ teaspoon thyme

½ teaspoon paprika

2 tablespoons fresh chopped parsley

For the yogurt garlic sauce

1 teaspoon olive oil

1 teaspoon minced garlic

2 cups plain yogurt

1 teaspoon chopped fresh parsley

Sea salt, for seasoning

To make the fatteh

1. Put the chickpeas in a large serving bowl along with the toasted pita, pine nuts, and almonds.

2. Heat the olive oil in a large skillet over medium-high heat and sauté the chicken breast, garlic powder, cardamom, coriander, thyme, and paprika until the meat is cooked through and coated in the spices, about 20 minutes.

3. Shred the chicken with a fork and add it to the bowl with the chickpeas, pita, and nuts.

4. Top with parsley.

To make the yogurt garlic sauce

1. While the chicken is cooking, heat the oil in a small saucepan over medium heat and sauté the garlic until fragrant, about 3 minutes. Stir in the yogurt and heat for 5 minutes.

2. Add the parsley to the yogurt sauce, season with salt, and set aside.

3. Drizzle the yogurt sauce over the fatteh.

4. Serve immediately.

FUN FACT: Pine nuts can take anywhere from 18 months to 3 years to mature enough to be harvested.

Iraqi Slow Cooked Chicken and Rice (Tbit)

SERVES 4 ♦ **PREP TIME:** 15 minutes ♦ **COOK TIME:** 8 to 9 hours

A slow cooker is a perfect appliance in which to create this traditional meal because it is supposed to cook all night. You can also use drumsticks in the recipe—just take care when eating the meal because the chicken gets so tender it falls off the bones.

2 tablespoons olive oil, plus extra for greasing the insert

1 pound boneless chicken thighs

1 (15-ounce) can low-sodium diced tomatoes

1 cup low-sodium chicken broth

1 sweet onion, chopped

½ cup raisins

2 teaspoons minced garlic

½ teaspoon ground nutmeg

½ teaspoon ground cinnamon

¼ teaspoon sea salt

⅛ teaspoon freshly ground black pepper

1 cup long-grain rice

1¾ cups water

1. Lightly grease the insert of a slow cooker with oil and set aside.

2. Heat the oil in a large skillet over medium-high heat and brown the chicken on all sides, about 10 minutes.

3. Add the tomatoes, broth, onion, raisins, garlic, nutmeg, cinnamon, salt, and pepper to the slow cooker insert.

4. Add the chicken thighs to the slow cooker and stir to combine.

5. Cover and cook on low for 8 to 9 hours.

6. When you are almost ready to eat, stir together the rice and water in a large saucepan over medium-high heat. Bring to a boil, then reduce the heat to low, cover, and simmer until the rice is tender and the liquid is absorbed, about 25 minutes.

7. Serve the chicken over the rice.

COOKING TIP: You can also make this dish in a stockpot on the stovetop. Brown the chicken, add the remaining ingredients to the pot, and simmer until the thighs are tender, about 1 hour.

Date-Filled
Cookies
(Maamoul),
page 128

Chapter Seven

DESSERTS

I n the Middle East and North Africa, sweets and desserts are important, and recipes are made with care to produce truly delectable creations. There is no such thing as low-fat or low-carb in traditional desserts, so dive in and enjoy the buttery pastries, rich cookies, and scrumptious puddings. Sweets are often linked to festivals and special occasions, so the finished product is lavish, decadent, and perfect when you need a lift in your spirits.

Baklava

SERVES 8 ♦ **PREP TIME:** 35 minutes, plus cooling time ♦ **COOK TIME:** 45 minutes

Do not be scared away by the length of this recipe; it is easier than it looks and well worth the effort. You will be making a delicious honey syrup and a warmly spiced nut mixture and layering store-bought phyllo pastry with lots of butter. Once you make baklava, it might become the dessert you show off at every function.

4½ cups finely chopped walnuts or pecans

1 teaspoon ground cinnamon

20 (9-by-13-inch or larger) sheets phyllo pastry

1 cup unsalted butter, melted

1 cup water

1 cup sugar

1 cup honey

2 tablespoons butter

⅛ teaspoon ground cloves

1. In a medium bowl, mix together the walnuts and cinnamon and set aside.

2. Preheat the oven to 350°F.

3. Take the phyllo pastry out of the package and lay it out in a stack. Use kitchen scissors to trim the sheets to fit a 9-by-13-inch deep baking dish. Discard the trimmings.

4. Brush the sides and bottom of the baking dish with melted butter.

5. Layer 5 phyllo sheets in the baking dish, buttering each sheet generously before topping it with another sheet.

6. Spread 1⅓ cups of the nut mixture over the top sheet, pressing down lightly with your hand to flatten.

7. Layer another 5 phyllo sheets in the baking dish, buttering each sheet generously before topping it with another sheet.

8. Spread 1⅓ cups of the nut mixture over the top sheet, pressing down lightly with your hand to flatten.

9. Layer 5 phyllo sheets in the baking dish, buttering each sheet generously before topping it with another sheet.

10. Spread 1⅓ cups of the nut mixture over the top sheet, pressing down lightly with your hand to flatten. Set the remaining nut mixture aside.

11. Top the last nut layer with the remaining 5 phyllo sheets, buttering each sheet generously before topping it with another sheet.

12. Place the baking dish in the freezer for 10 minutes to firm up the dessert.

13. Score the top layer of phyllo in a diagonal crosshatch pattern with a sharp knife to create squares about 1½ inches wide.

14. Bake until golden brown, 40 to 45 minutes.

15. While the baklava is baking, stir together the water, sugar, honey, butter, and cloves in a medium saucepan over medium-high heat. Bring to a boil, reduce the heat to low, and simmer for 5 to 7 minutes to dissolve the sugar. Set aside.

16. Remove the baklava from the oven and pour the syrup over it evenly. Sprinkle the remaining ½ cup walnut mixture over the top.

17. Let the baklava sit for 4 to 6 hours to cool and settle, then slice and serve.

18. Leftovers can be stored in the refrigerator for up to 1 week.

VARIATION TIP: Hazelnuts and pistachios are common in Turkey, and in Iran rose water often flavors the flaky, sweet layers.

Date-Filled Cookies (Maamoul)

SERVES 4 ♦ **PREP TIME:** 30 minutes ♦ **COOK TIME:** 15 minutes

If you enjoy Fig Newton cookies, you will love these rich, lightly spiced filled cookies. They are so easy to make and they freeze beautifully. Maamoul are traditional offerings at religious holidays, such as Eid at the end of Ramadan in Syria, Jordan, Israel, and Lebanon. However, you can enjoy them anytime!

¾ cup melted butter or ghee
3 tablespoons sugar
Pinch ground cinnamon

2¼ cups all-purpose flour, plus more if necessary
¼ cup whole milk, plus more if necessary

¾ pound Medjool whole dates or date paste

1. Preheat the oven to 350°F.
2. Line a baking sheet with parchment paper and set aside.
3. In a large bowl, mix together the butter, sugar, and cinnamon until blended.
4. Add the flour and mix the ingredients together until the mixture looks like coarse crumbs.
5. Add half the milk and mix it into the other ingredients, using your fingers. Then add the remaining milk 1 tablespoon at a time until a smooth dough is formed. Knead the dough in the bowl until it is pliable and not sticky. Let the dough rest for 30 minutes.
6. While the dough is resting, put the dates in a food processor and pulse until smooth and spreadable.
7. Roll the dough into 34 balls of relatively equal size.
8. Pick up a dough ball and flatten it into a round ¼ inch thick, then scoop about 1 scant tablespoon of filling into the center.
9. Fold the dough over to form a half-moon shape and pinch the edges together to seal the cookie. Flatten the cookie slightly and place it on the baking sheet.
10. Repeat with the remaining dough and filling, spacing the cookies about 1½ inches apart.

11. Bake until light brown, about 15 minutes.

12. Cool the cookies and store for up to 1 week in a sealed container at room temperature.

COOKING TIP: Try to find a traditional maamoul mold and use that instead of creating the half-moon shapes in this recipe. You arrange rolled dough on both sides of the mold and fill one with the date paste. Then you fold the mold over, and a sealed, imprinted cookie pops out.

Lebanese Rice Pudding with Pistachio (Ruz ib Haleeb)

SERVES 4 ♦ **PREP TIME:** 10 minutes ♦ **COOK TIME:** 25 minutes

Rice pudding will probably be one of the more familiar dishes in this book, as it is made in different variations all over the world. The difference with Lebanese rice pudding lies in the subtle orange flavor and crunchy pistachio topping. Add a pinch of cloves or allspice to perk up the taste even more.

2 cups whole milk, plus more if needed

⅓ cup sugar, or more for a sweeter flavor

1 cup long-grain rice

Juice and zest of ½ orange

½ cup chopped pistachios, for garnish

1. Stir together the milk, sugar, rice, orange juice, and orange zest in a large saucepan over medium-high heat.

2. Bring to a boil, then reduce the heat to low and simmer until the rice is very tender and the liquid is absorbed, about 25 minutes. Add more milk if the pudding is too thick.

3. Remove the pudding from the heat and pour into a serving dish. Cover the top with plastic wrap, pressing it to the surface of the pudding, and chill completely in the refrigerator.

4. Serve topped with pistachios.

COOKING TIP: You can also bake this pudding if you do not want to supervise the cooking process. In a medium mixing bowl, add 2 large eggs to the unheated milk mixture and stir in cooked rice. Transfer to a greased casserole dish and bake at 350°F until tender and thick, about 45 minutes.

Persian Walnut Cookies (Nan-e gerdui)

SERVES 4 ♦ **PREP TIME:** 20 minutes ♦ **COOK TIME:** 15 minutes

The ground nut base of these cookies is gluten-free and creates a glorious chewy texture and rich taste. You can add a splash of rose water if you enjoy it (and can find it at the store). Add a walnut half on top of each cookie before baking for a fancier presentation.

1 cup walnut pieces
  or halves
3 large egg yolks

¼ cup sugar
1 teaspoon vanilla extract

¼ teaspoon ground
  cinnamon

1. Preheat the oven to 300°F and line a baking sheet with parchment paper.

2. Put the walnuts in a food processor and pulse until finely ground.

3. In a medium bowl, beat together the egg yolks, sugar, vanilla, and cinnamon with a handheld electric beater until pale and thick, 4 to 5 minutes.

4. Fold the ground walnuts into the egg yolk mixture until well combined.

5. Drop the batter by teaspoons onto the baking sheet with about 1½ inches between the cookies. Spread the dough slightly with the back of the spoon and bake them until they are light brown, about 15 minutes.

6. Cool on the sheet, then store in a container at room temperature for up to 5 days.

FUN FACT: Walnuts are the oldest tree food on record, dating back from before 9000 BCE by some records. This nut was transported all over the world as a valuable trade commodity, as it stays fresh as long as you leave the flesh in the shell.

Toasted Semolina Pudding (Mamounieh)

SERVES 4 ♦ **PREP TIME:** 15 minutes ♦ **COOK TIME:** 14 minutes

Of all the desserts in this book, this one might be the most unusual. The texture is similar to cream of wheat, but the flavor is sweet and toasty with a hint of butter and cinnamon. It is ideal when you want a special treat or something different.

4 cups water

2 cups sugar

3 tablespoons butter

1 cup semolina

Ground cinnamon, for garnish

½ cup chopped, roasted pistachios, for garnish

1. In a medium saucepan, stir together the water and sugar and place over medium-high heat. Bring to a boil, then reduce the heat to low and let the mixture simmer until thickened, about 10 minutes.

2. While cooking the water and sugar mixture, melt the butter in a large saucepan over medium-high heat.

3. Stir in the semolina and toast it, stirring constantly, until golden brown and fragrant, about 4 minutes.

4. Slowly pour the sugar mixture into the toasted semolina, stirring constantly, and let the pudding simmer for a few minutes to incorporate the liquid.

5. Spoon the pudding into serving bowls and top with a sprinkle of cinnamon and pistachios.

6. Serve warm.

VARIATION TIP: The Lebanese version of this dessert includes crushed pistachios or pistachio powder, as well as yogurt and coconut.

Turkish Delight

SERVES 8 ♦ **PREP TIME:** 30 minutes, plus chilling time ♦ **COOK TIME:** 15 minutes

Turkish Delight has a long history stretching back to 18th-century Istanbul. This might look like a complicated recipe, but after the sugar syrup is made, it is basically just stirring the other ingredients in and waiting to eat the treat.

1 cup powdered sugar

¼ cup cornstarch

Vegetable oil, for greasing
  the baking dish

2 cups sugar

1¼ cups water, divided

1 tablespoon lemon juice

1 teaspoon cream of tartar

2 tablespoons
  gelatin powder

1 tablespoon rose water

2 or 3 drops red
  food coloring

1. In a small bowl, stir together the powdered sugar and cornstarch.

2. Lightly oil a 9-by-9-inch baking dish with oil and dust it with a tablespoon or two of the icing sugar and cornstarch mixture. Tap out any excess and set the baking dish aside.

3. In a large saucepan over medium-high heat, stir together the sugar, ½ cup water, the lemon juice, and the cream of tartar. Bring the mixture to a boil, reduce the heat to medium-low, and simmer until the mixture reaches 125°F on a candy thermometer, 12 to 15 minutes. Then remove from the heat and set aside.

4. In a small saucepan, bring ¼ cup of water to a boil over high heat, remove from the heat, and whisk in the gelatin until dissolved.

5. Whisk in the remaining ½ cup of water, the rose water, and the food coloring. Then whisk the gelatin mixture into the sugar syrup mixture.

6. Pour the Turkish delight into the prepared baking dish and refrigerate for 6 hours to set.

7. Remove the candy from the dish and cut into 1-inch pieces. Coat them in the icing sugar mixture. Store in a covered container for up to 1 week.

FUN FACT: This dessert is the inspiration for the gummy sweet center of jelly beans.

Bread Pudding (Umm Ali)

SERVES 8 ♦ **PREP TIME:** 30 minutes ♦ **COOK TIME:** 40 minutes

Umm Ali is an Egyptian national dish whose name translates to "Ali's Mother." Try topping the dessert with a dollop of whipped cream or scoop of vanilla ice cream.

Oil, for greasing a baking dish

1 (17-ounce) package frozen puff pastry

1 cup chopped pistachios

1 cup slivered almonds

1 cup shredded coconut

2 cups water

1 (14-ounce) can sweetened condensed milk

1 teaspoon pure vanilla extract

½ cup heavy (whipping) cream

1. Preheat the oven to 400°F.

2. Lightly oil a 9-by-13-inch baking dish and set aside.

3. Line a baking sheet with parchment paper and arrange the frozen puff pastry sheets on it.

4. Bake the pastry until golden and puffed, 12 to 15 minutes.

5. Cut or break the puff pastry into 1-inch pieces and transfer them to a large bowl.

6. Add the pistachios, almonds, and coconut and toss to combine.

7. Transfer the mixture to the baking dish, spreading it out evenly.

8. In a medium saucepan, heat the water, sweetened condensed milk, and vanilla over medium-high heat.

9. Bring to a boil and reduce the heat to low and simmer 7 to 10 minutes.

10. Remove the mixture from the heat and cool for 30 minutes.

11. Pour the milk mixture into the baking dish and let stand for 10 minutes. Pour the cream over the bread mixture and bake until golden, about 15 minutes.

12. Let the bread pudding cool for 10 minutes and serve.

VARIATION TIP: For a less traditional version of this dessert you can use regular bread, pastry, or leftover croissant in place of the puff pastry. Use the same amount as the puff pastry and follow the recipe as written.

Kanafeh

SERVES 8 ♦ **PREP TIME:** 30 minutes ♦ **COOK TIME:** 42 minutes

My mother referred to this dish as "delicious but fiddly." To be fair, she used a very complicated traditional recipe, so I have tried to simplify the dish so that you can enjoy it whenever you need a distinctive dessert.

For the simple syrup

1 cup water

1¼ cups sugar

Juice of ½ lemon

2 tablespoons rose water (optional)

For the pastry

12 ounces frozen phyllo pastry

¾ cup melted butter

12 ounces shredded mozzarella cheese

8 ounces ricotta cheese

½ cup chopped pistachios

To make the simple syrup

1. In a medium saucepan, stir together the water and sugar and bring to a boil over high heat. Reduce the heat to low and simmer for 5 to 7 minutes to thicken slightly.

2. Remove from the heat and stir in the lemon juice and rose water (if using). Set aside to cool.

To make the pastry

1. Preheat the oven to 375°F.

2. Put the frozen pastry in a food processor and pulse until it is shredded. Transfer the shredded pastry to a large bowl.

3. Add the melted butter and toss with your hands to coat the shredded pastry completely.

4. In a medium bowl, stir together the mozzarella and ricotta until well blended.

5. Spread half of the pastry mixture in the bottom of a 9-by-13-inch baking dish, pressing down firmly.

6. Spread the cheese mixture evenly over the pastry layer and top with the remaining shredded pastry, covering the cheese completely.

CONTINUED ▶

7. Bake until the pastry is golden brown and crispy, 30 to 35 minutes.

8. Let the pastry cool for 10 minutes, then remove it from the baking dish after running a knife around the edges.

9. Pour the simple syrup over the pastry evenly and sprinkle with pistachios.

10. Serve warm and store any leftovers in the refrigerator, covered, for up to 3 days.

FUN FACT: Rose water is made from distilled buds, stems, and petals and is very popular in Arab recipes, as well as for other applications.

Sesame Candies (Halvah)

MAKES 64 ♦ **PREP TIME:** 20 minutes, plus chilling time ♦ **COOK TIME:** 10 minutes

These are kind of like a sesame-flavored fudge, with a pleasing hint of spice and vanilla. Without the need for a candy thermometer, you will find the texture of this version crumblier and less velvety than that of the other labor-intensive versions of this treat.

Butter, for greasing the baking dish	2 cups tahini paste	¼ teaspoon ground cinnamon
2 cups sugar	Juice of ½ lemon	⅛ teaspoon ground nutmeg
½ cup water	1 teaspoon pure vanilla extract	Pinch ground allspice

1. Lightly grease an 8-by-8-inch baking pan with butter and set aside.

2. Stir together the sugar and water in a medium saucepan and place it over medium heat. Bring to a boil, reduce the heat to low, and simmer until the sugar syrup is thickened and coats the back of a spoon, about 10 minutes. Do not stir it while it simmers.

3. Remove the syrup from the heat and set aside to cool for 10 minutes.

4. In a large bowl, stir together the tahini, lemon juice, vanilla, cinnamon, nutmeg, and allspice until smooth and well blended.

5. Add the sugar syrup to the tahini mixture and stir together as quickly as possible until well mixed. Then pour the mixture into the prepared baking dish.

6. Cool completely, cover with plastic wrap, and set in the refrigerator for at least 24 hours to set completely.

7. Cut into 1-inch squares and store in the refrigerator in a sealed container for up to 1 week.

FUN FACT: Caramel was originally used by women to remove unwanted hair.

Milk Pudding (Mahalabia)

SERVES 4 ◆ **PREP TIME:** 10 minutes, plus chilling time ◆ **COOK TIME:** 10 minutes

This recipe is a variation of custard, a popular dessert in many countries. Hints of orange, crunchy toasted nuts, and warm cardamom enhance the lush, smooth custard, creating an elegant dessert perfect for special guests.

2½ cups whole milk, divided
¼ cup cornstarch
1 (12-ounce) can
   evaporated milk

¾ cup sugar
½ tablespoon orange zest or
   orange water

¼ teaspoon ground
   cardamom
½ cup slivered,
   toasted almonds

1. In a small bowl, whisk together ½ cup milk and the cornstarch until lump-free.

2. In a large, heavy-bottomed saucepan, whisk together the remaining 2 cups of milk, evaporated milk, sugar, orange zest, and cardamom. Then, whisk in the cornstarch mixture.

3. Place the saucepan over medium heat and bring to a boil, stirring frequently. Reduce the heat to low and simmer until the mixture resembles thick custard, about 10 minutes.

4. Remove the custard from the heat and spoon it into a serving bowl or individual serving bowls. Cover with plastic wrap, ensuring the plastic is pressed snugly on the top of the pudding to prevent a skin. Refrigerate until completely chilled.

5. Serve topped with toasted almonds.

VARIATION TIP: The Israeli version of Mahalabia includes rose water and often replaces the milk with grape juice to conform to religious laws.

Schug (Zhug),
page 144

Chapter Eight

SAUCES AND SPICE BLENDS

Many Middle Eastern dishes depend on, or are enhanced by, sauces, spice mixes, and toppings. Using some spice blends or a drizzle of tahini sauce on your "regular" recipes is an excellent way to experiment with Middle Eastern flavors. Try rubbing shawarma spice on chicken before grilling it, or spoon schug on a wrap if you like your meals hot and spicy. Be creative!

Tahini Sauce

MAKES 1 cup ♦ **PREP TIME:** 10 minutes

Tahini sauce can be used on almost anything. Drizzle it on vegetables, meats, rice, or couscous, and use it as a tasty spread for sandwiches or stuffed pitas. The rich sesame and garlic flavors are sharpened by lemon juice and a hint of salt.

½ cup tahini

½ cup water

Juice of ½ lemon

2 teaspoons minced garlic

Sea salt

1. Put the tahini, water, lemon juice, and garlic in a blender and blend until smooth and pale, about 1 minute, scraping down the sides at least once.

2. Transfer the sauce to a container and season with salt.

3. Store, covered, in the refrigerator for up to 1 week.

FUN FACT: When tasty little sesame seeds ripen, they come out of the pods with an audible pop—which inspired the famous phrase "open sesame."

Lebanese Garlic Sauce (Toum)

MAKES 2 cups ♦ **PREP TIME:** 10 minutes

Toum is essentially a garlic mayonnaise or aioli. Try it with grilled chicken or Middle Eastern Lamb Kebabs (page 105), drizzle it on Falafel (page 28), or even toss it with robust romaine leaves as a delicious salad. You can mellow and sweeten the garlic flavor by roasting the cloves first.

20 to 25 peeled garlic cloves

½ teaspoon sea salt, plus extra for seasoning

Juice of ½ lemon, divided

1½ to 2 cups grapeseed oil, divided

2 tablespoons ice water

1. Put the garlic and salt in a blender or food processor and pulse, scraping down the sides with a spatula, until the garlic is very finely chopped.

2. Add half the lemon juice and process until the garlic and juice form a smooth paste.

3. Keep the blender or processor running and slowly add half the oil in a thin stream along with the remaining lemon juice. Then drizzle in the remaining oil with the water until the sauce is thick and emulsified.

4. Store the sauce in a sealed container in the refrigerator for up to 2 weeks.

VARIATION TIP: Some cooks add about 2 tablespoons of fresh mint to this pungent sauce to boost the flavor. If you do so, add the mint in the first step while adding the garlic.

Schug (Zhug)

MAKES 1 cup ♦ **PREP TIME:** 20 minutes

Schug, or zhug, is Yemeni in origin, and the bright, intense flavor comes from a generous amount of hot peppers. The green herbs provide a lovely color, as well as different flavor notes besides hot.

8 jalapeño peppers, seeded and sliced

½ bunch fresh parsley, coarsely chopped

½ bunch fresh cilantro, coarsely chopped

1½ tablespoons minced garlic

1 tablespoon olive oil

¼ teaspoon ground cumin

¼ teaspoon ground cardamom

Pinch ground cinnamon

Pinch ground nutmeg

Pinch freshly ground black pepper

Sea salt

1. Put the jalapeño peppers, parsley, cilantro, garlic, olive oil, cumin, cardamom, cinnamon, nutmeg, and black pepper in a food processor and process, scraping down the sides with a spatula, until the mixture is a rough paste with a pesto-like consistency.

2. Transfer the mixture to a container and season with salt. Store the sauce, covered, in the refrigerator for up to 5 days, or in the freezer in a covered ice cube tray for up to 1 month.

MENU TIP: Try freezing the sauce in ice cube trays. Then, simply pop the frozen cube in your recipe, directly from the freezer.

Crispy Fried Onions

MAKES 1 cup ♦ **PREP TIME:** 10 minutes ♦ **COOK TIME:** 40 minutes

When onions are sautéed slowly, the natural sugars in the allium caramelize to create intense favor and a deep golden color. Make sure you do not slice the onions too thin, or they can burn. Use a large enough skillet so that the onions aren't crowded, or they will steam, which purges water and makes this process take much longer.

½ cup olive oil

3 large sweet onions, (about 1 pound), cut into ⅛-inch slices

1. Heat the oil in a large skillet over medium-high heat until water sizzles when drops are added to the skillet.
2. Add the onions and cook, stirring, until the onions start to sweat. Then reduce the heat to medium and cook, stirring frequently, until the onions are golden brown and crispy, 35 to 40 minutes.
3. Use immediately or store the onions in a sealed container in the refrigerator for up to 4 days. Reheat the onions in a skillet when you want to use them.

FUN FACT: In ancient Egypt, onions were used in burial rituals because their rings and shape were considered symbols of eternity.

Za'atar

MAKES ¼ cup ♦ **PREP TIME:** 10 minutes ♦ **COOK TIME:** 10 minutes

Za'atar means "thyme" in Arabic. The recipe also contains an ingredient (sumac) that you might have to search for online or in specialty markets. It is really not optional here. You may also be able to find a less potent and less flavorful za'atar seasoning in the spice section of most grocery stores, but it is always preferable to make it yourself.

½ cup fresh thyme leaves	1 tablespoon sesame seeds	Sea salt
1 tablespoon sumac	2 teaspoons dried marjoram	

1. Preheat the oven to 300°F.
2. Line a small baking sheet with parchment paper and spread the thyme on the sheet.
3. Bake until the thyme is just dried out, about 10 minutes.
4. Let the thyme cool, then grind it finely in a coffee or spice grinder or with a mortar and pestle along with the sumac.
5. Transfer the thyme-sumac mixture to a container, stir in the sesame seeds and marjoram, and season with salt.
6. Store, covered, in the refrigerator for up to 1 week, or in the freezer for up to 1 month.

VARIATION TIP: Za'atar spice mixtures can include dried oregano, nutmeg, cumin, coriander, and red pepper flakes, depending on your preference.

Middle Eastern Spice Blend (Bahārāt)

MAKES ⅓ cup ♦ **PREP TIME:** 10 minutes ♦ **COOK TIME:** 4 minutes

Bahārāt is Arabic for "spices." This recipe is just one version, and you can adjust the quantities of the spices to suit your own tastes. In a pinch, if you do not have a spice or coffee grinder, you can use ground spices.

4 teaspoons whole cumin seeds

4 teaspoons black peppercorns

2 teaspoons coriander seeds

1 teaspoon whole cloves

4 teaspoons paprika

1 teaspoon ground cinnamon

½ teaspoon ground cardamom

½ teaspoon ground nutmeg

1. Place a small skillet over medium-high heat and add the cumin, peppercorns, coriander, and cloves.

2. Roast the spices, swirling the skillet, until they are very fragrant, about 4 minutes.

3. Remove the skillet from the heat and transfer the spices to a coffee or spice grinder and let cool.

4. Add the paprika, cinnamon, cardamom, and nutmeg and grind all the spices together.

5. Transfer the blend to a container, cover, and store at room temperature out of direct sunlight for up to 2 weeks.

VARIATION TIP: In Turkey, a generous amount of mint is added to this blend. In North African countries, you might see rosebuds and a hint of cinnamon.

Harissa

MAKES 1 cup ♦ **PREP TIME:** 15 minutes, plus rehydrating time

My first taste of harissa started a lifetime love affair with this hot, complex, utterly delicious sauce. During my first trip to Libya, when I was 18 years old, we had to fly into Tunisia and drive across the border because planes from other countries were forbidden to land in Tripoli. We were hot and hungry, and when my dad stopped at a roadside stand, we probably would have eaten anything. The sandwich was tuna with pickled vegetables and a generous smear of a red sauce. Harissa!

8 large, dried medium-hot chile peppers

Juice of ½ lemon

2 teaspoons minced garlic

2 teaspoons tomato paste

1½ teaspoons smoked hot paprika

1 teaspoon apple cider vinegar

1 teaspoon ground coriander

1 teaspoon ground cumin

¼ teaspoon sea salt

2 tablespoons olive oil

1. Put the peppers in a medium bowl, cover with hot water, and set aside until rehydrated, about 20 minutes. Then remove the stems and seeds from the peppers and put the peppers in a food processor along with the lemon juice, garlic, tomato paste, paprika, vinegar, coriander, cumin, and salt.

2. Process, scraping down the sides with a spatula, until the ingredients form a smooth paste.

3. Keep the processor running and add the olive oil in a thin stream.

4. Transfer the harissa to a container with a lid and store in the refrigerator for up to 1 month, or spoon the harissa into an ice cube tray, cover, and freeze for up to 2 months.

VARIATION TIP: Mild guajillo chiles, slightly sweet ancho chiles, and medium-hot Kashmiri chiles are great options, either alone or in a blend.

Shawarma Spice

MAKES 9 tablespoons ♦ **PREP TIME:** 5 minutes

Seafood, beef, and chicken are all enhanced by this warm spice blend. You can also sprinkle it on flatbread, in soups or stews, and on vegetables, or use it to flavor a dip or sauce.

2 tablespoons garlic powder

2 tablespoons ground allspice

1 tablespoon ground cinnamon

1 tablespoon ground nutmeg

2 teaspoons freshly ground black pepper

2 teaspoons ground cloves

2 teaspoons ground cardamom

1 teaspoon ground oregano

1 teaspoon chili powder

1 teaspoon sea salt

1. In a small bowl, combine the garlic powder, allspice, cinnamon, nutmeg, pepper, cloves, cardamom, oregano, chili powder, and salt until well blended.

2. Transfer to a container or jar with a lid and store in a cool, dry place for up to 1 month.

Red Chile Pepper Paste (Shatta)

MAKES 1 cup ♦ **PREP TIME:** 10 minutes, plus draining time

The Middle East region features many different types of hot sauces, some complex and subtle, and others, like this one, just an exhilarating burst of heat. The paste-like consistency of shatta means it is very concentrated, so it should be portioned out conservatively.

10 red chile peppers, stemmed and seeded

Juice of 1 lemon
1 teaspoon sea salt

¼ cup olive oil

1. Put the peppers, lemon juice, and salt in a food processor and pulse until very finely chopped and almost paste-like.

2. Set a fine-mesh strainer over a bowl and transfer the pepper mixture to the strainer. Place the bowl in the refrigerator and leave the mixture to strain for 2 to 4 days, pressing gently with the back of a spoon every 12 hours or so to remove liquid.

3. Transfer the paste to a container with a lid and pour the olive oil on top in a thin layer. Store, covered, in the refrigerator for up to 1 week.

MENU TIP: Try serving this intensely flavored sauce with grilled beef, simple kebabs, and fluffy white rice or couscous.

Ras El Hanout

MAKES ¼ cup ♦ **PREP TIME:** 5 minutes

I first tried this spice blend while working as a chef in North Africa, and I was immediately smitten. The blend has all the familiar warm spices used in North American and European cuisine, combined in a new fragrant and slightly hot manner. I use it on everything, except perhaps my morning coffee.

3 teaspoons ground cumin

3 teaspoons ground ginger

1½ teaspoons sea salt

¾ teaspoon ground coriander

¾ teaspoon ground allspice

¾ teaspoon ground cinnamon

¾ teaspoon cayenne pepper

¾ teaspoon freshly ground black pepper

¾ teaspoon ground cloves

1. In a small bowl, combine the cumin, ginger, salt, coriander, allspice, cinnamon, cayenne, black pepper, and cloves until well blended.

2. Transfer the spice blend to a container with a lid and store in a cool, dry place for up to 1 month.

VARIATION TIP: This North African staple is a combination of many high-quality spices, and its name means "top of the shop." You could also use mace, nutmeg, fenugreek, fennel seed, or aniseed.

MEASUREMENT CONVERSIONS

	US STANDARD	US STANDARD (OUNCES)	METRIC (APPROXIMATE)
VOLUME EQUIVALENTS (LIQUID)	2 tablespoons	1 fl. oz.	30 mL
	¼ cup	2 fl. oz.	60 mL
	½ cup	4 fl. oz.	120 mL
	1 cup	8 fl. oz.	240 mL
	1½ cups	12 fl. oz.	355 mL
	2 cups or 1 pint	16 fl. oz.	475 mL
	4 cups or 1 quart	32 fl. oz.	1 L
	1 gallon	128 fl. oz.	4 L
VOLUME EQUIVALENTS (DRY)	⅛ teaspoon	—	0.5 mL
	¼ teaspoon	—	1 mL
	½ teaspoon	—	2 mL
	¾ teaspoon	—	4 mL
	1 teaspoon	—	5 mL
	1 tablespoon	—	15 mL
	¼ cup	—	59 mL
	⅓ cup	—	79 mL
	½ cup	—	118 mL
	⅔ cup	—	156 mL
	¾ cup	—	177 mL
	1 cup	—	235 mL
	2 cups or 1 pint	—	475 mL
	3 cups	—	700 mL
	4 cups or 1 quart	—	1 L
	½ gallon	—	2 L
	1 gallon	—	4 L
WEIGHT EQUIVALENTS	½ ounce	—	15 g
	1 ounce	—	30 g
	2 ounces	—	60 g
	4 ounces	—	115 g
	8 ounces	—	225 g
	12 ounces	—	340 g
	16 ounces or 1 pound	—	455 g

	FAHRENHEIT (F)	CELSIUS (C) (APPROXIMATE)
OVEN TEMPERATURES	250°F	120°C
	300°F	150°C
	325°F	180°C
	375°F	190°C
	400°F	200°C
	425°F	220°C
	450°F	230°C

RESOURCES

In many communities, Middle Eastern or international markets are not part of the shopping choices, so it is fortunate that many ingredients and spices are available online. The following sites are offered as possibilities, but you are encouraged to search out local options, as well.

SILKROADSPICES.CA

HASHEMS.COM

ZAMOURISPICES.COM

PERSIANBASKET.COM

IGOURMET.COM/MIDDLEEASTERNFOOD.ASP

BUYLEBANESE.COM

KALAMALA.COM

THESPICETRADER.CA

SEASONEDPIONEERS.COM

INDEX

ACKNOWLEDGMENTS

Thank you to my father, who allowed me to experience other cultures through his incredible career and years spent in the Middle East. And thank you to my mother, who threw herself wholeheartedly into local customs and cuisine and who never met a person she did not want to talk to or learn from, even if they did not speak her language!

I am grateful to the Callisto Media team for their incredible hard work and for giving me the opportunity to work on more than 30 books with them over the years. They have helped me become a better writer.

Thank you to all the chefs, suppliers, farmers, and home cooks over the last 30 years who contributed to my knowledge of food and imparted their passion for exceptional ingredients and wonderful recipes.

ABOUT THE AUTHOR

 **Michelle Anderson** is the author and ghostwriter of more than 30 cookbooks focused on healthy diets and delicious food. She worked as a professional chef for over 25 years, honing her craft overseas in North Africa and all over Ontario, Canada, in fine dining restaurants. She worked as a corporate executive chef for Rational Canada for 4 years, collaborating with her international counterparts and consulting in kitchens all over Southern Ontario and in the United States. Michelle ran her own catering company and personal chef business and was a wedding cake designer, as well. Her focus was food as medicine and using field-to-fork wholesome quality ingredients in vibrant visually impactful dishes. Michelle lives in Temiskaming Shores, Ontario, Canada, with her husband, two sons, two Newfoundland dogs, and three cats.

Printed in the USA
CPSIA information can be obtained
at www.ICGtesting.com
LVHW052136091223
765798LV00002B/28